TEEN SPIRIT

ONE WORLD, MANY PATHS

your guide to spirituality & religion

PAUL B. RAUSHENBUSH

Health Communications, Inc.
Deerfield Beach, Florida

www.hcibooks.com

Library of Congress Cataloging-in-Publication Data

Raushenbush, Paul B.
    Teen spirit : one world, many paths : your guide to spirituality & religion / Paul B.
    Raushenbush
        p.   cm.
    Includes bibliographical references.
    ISBN 0-7373-0119-3
       1. Religions.   2. Teenagers—Religious life.   I. Title.

BL80.3.R38 2004
200'.835—dc22

2004052358

Publisher: HCI Teens
             An Imprint of Health Communications, Inc.
             3201 S.W. 15th Street
             Deerfield Beach, FL 33442–8190

Cover design by Andrea Perrine Brower
Inside book design by Lawna Patterson Oldfield

TO MY PARENTS,

MARYLU DEWATTEVILLE RAUSHENBUSH

AND WALTER BRANDEIS RAUSHENBUSH,

AND TO GOD WHO IS LOVE.

CONTENTS

Q&A WITH PASTOR PAUL

PASTOR PAUL'S TIPS FOR SPIRITUAL SEEKERS

JUST THE FAQS

WHY I'M . . .

QUIZZES

What The Religions Say About

. . . AND OTHER STUFF

Celebrity Spirituality

INTERFAITH FOCUS

APPENDIX

WHERE TO GO FOR MORE INFORMATION

ACKNOWLEDGMENTS

This book is the result of help and encouragement from family, friends, colleagues and students. Very special thanks to my friend Brad Gooch for his advice and support. Enormous thanks to my *www.Beliefnet.com* editor and friend Paul O'Donnell, as well as to the other wonderful and hugely helpful past and present staffers from *www.Beliefnet.com* who made this book possible such as Rebecca Phillips, Laura Sheahen, Ellen Leventry, Elizabeth Sams, Steve Waldman, Debbie Caldwell, Mary Talbot, Anne Simpkinson, Rhonda Roumani, Arun Venugopal and Mark Tauber. Thank you for the generosity of the *www.Beliefnet.com* staff and writers for giving me permission to reprint the *www.Beliefnet.com* celebrity interviews. A special thanks to Anthony DeCurtis for his generosity and inspiration.

I also thank the University of North Carolina National Study of Youth and Religion (*www.youthandreligion.org*) and the UCLA Study on Spirituality in Higher Education (*www.spirituality.ucla.edu*) for the Faith Facts used in this book.

Thanks to the young people who wrote the essays for Teen Spirit—your pieces are the best reading in this book. Thanks to my friends throughout Princeton University, especially in the Office of Religious Life and the Religious Life Council, for being so inspiring and making me feel welcome. Thanks to Rev. Michael Easterling, Rev. Dr. Rodney Romney and Rev. Dr. James A. Forbes Jr. for being wonderful pastoral models for me. Thanks to the great people at Health Communications—especially my editor Elisabeth Rinaldi, and to my fun and effective agent Claudia Cross at Sterling, Lord Literistic.

Finally, thanks to my family for showing me how to laugh and to live life fully by surrounding me with love.

PREFACE

What do you believe?

All of us believe in something. You, your best friend, your worst enemy and that person you passed by on the street—all of us have some religious background or belief about spirituality. Our beliefs help us understand how the world works and help us with our choices about how to live in the world. Our beliefs are what make us both unique individuals as well as part of the human race.

Maybe you believe in the religious tradition that your parents handed down to you—or maybe you are resisting it with all your might. Your new girlfriend or boyfriend may be spiritual but not religious because she or he distrusts organized religion. Your teammate might even be agnostic or atheist and feel that religious people are out of their minds. Your coach might believe in his religion and be convinced that he is right and others are just plain wrong. Or maybe you know someone who defines things in their own way, like the musician Moby, who told me in an interview, "As much as I love Christ and the teachings of Christ, I can't call myself a Christian, because to call yourself a Christian implies a certainty that I don't have."

So, what do you believe?

Your answer is the starting point for this book. When you begin a journey, you need to know where you've started to really understand where you're going—even if that means coming back to the same starting point a little wiser and more knowledgeable. Think of this book as a map to find your own path through the sometimes unfamiliar but always exciting landscape of spirituality in your life and religion in America.

Whatever you believe, there has never been a better opportunity to explore your spirituality than right now and right here. In the United States, more religious traditions live side by side than in any other country in the world. You already hang out with people who have beliefs different from your own—on the soccer field, in coffeehouses, at concerts and in college. But we don't always know much about each other's beliefs, or else we assume things that aren't true.

What does my neighbor believe?

Bono, from the rock group U2, touched on the human longing to understand life when he sang, "I still haven't found what I'm looking for" on the album *Joshua Tree*. All of us search for answers to the big questions: What force governs the universe? What is the purpose for my life? Why do death and sadness exist? What is love? What moral code should guide my actions? Religions and spiritual beliefs provide a variety of different answers to these questions. Understanding how religions are different from each other is as important as knowing how they are similar.

When I visited a Greek Orthodox church while writing this book, one of my favorite things was the presbyter (priest) saying, "Be attentive!" before any reading from the Bible. My wish for you while reading this book is "Be attentive." Stay open and aware that you are learning sacred knowledge which has been passed down through the ages. Be attentive—and know that you have within you many of the answers you seek. Be attentive—and I guarantee that by the end of the book you will be better able to answer the questions, "What does my neighbor believe?" and "What do I believe?" These are two of the most exciting and important questions we can answer in this lifetime. Your personal answers will be an important and crucial addition to the already wonderful tapestry of belief that is the spiritual fabric of America.

NOTE: *I have focused on the five most influential world religions: Buddhism, Christianity, Hinduism, Islam and Judaism. While I have tried to be inclusive in this book by adding voices from young practitioners of several other religions, there are important traditions that are missing such as Taoism, Shinto, Confucianism and African Diaspora religions such as Santeria and Rastafarianism. Hopefully, as America grows more religiously diverse, future editions of this book will cover an even wider range of religious traditions.*

FREEDOM OF RELIGION

In 1788, the U.S. Constitution was ratified with the preamble as follows:

"We the People of the United States, in Order to form a more perfect Union, establish Justice, insure domestic Tranquility, provide for the common defense, promote the general Welfare, and secure the Blessings of Liberty to ourselves and our Posterity, do ordain and establish this Constitution for the United States of America."

In 1791 the First Amendment was ratified, stating that the government will not establish one official religion, and that we may have freedom to practice our own religion—whatever that may be. The First Amendment, guaranteeing freedom of religion, press and expression, was ratified on December 15, 1791. It reads:

"Congress shall make no law respecting an establishment of religion, or prohibiting the free exercise thereof; or abridging the freedom of speech, or of the press; or the right of the people peaceably to assemble, and to petition the Government for a redress of grievances."

In 1948 the General Assembly of the United Nations adopted and proclaimed the Universal Declaration of Human Rights. Article 18 deals specifically with freedom of religion:

"Everyone has the right to freedom of thought, conscience and religion; this right includes freedom to change his religion or belief, and

freedom, either alone or in community with others and in public or private, to manifest his religion or belief in teaching, practice, worship and observance."

INTRODUCTION

What do I believe?

During an interview for my current position as associate dean of religious life at Princeton University, a student asked me how I balanced being a Christian minister with my interest and appreciation for all different religions. It was a good question and one that is often asked of me.

Like a geologist fascinated by rocks, or a botanist who can't get enough of plants, I love people. And since religions are, in the end, not made up of rules and beliefs but made up of *people* who follow those rules and believe together, nothing is more fascinating to me than religious people. That doesn't mean I believe every religion I encounter. Rather, I love to learn about someone else's beliefs as a way to know and understand them more deeply.

I'm interfaith myself. My grandmother on my father's side was Jewish, so while I was raised Christian, I grew up with my Jewish cousins. We occasionally argued about who was a better tennis player, but it never occurred to us that one of our religions was "better" than the other, only different. In my family, we were taught that difference was good because it made life more interesting. As an adult, I continue to value and respect other religions.

My feelings of patriotism also propel me to learn about other religions. I believe in the American ideals of equality, democracy, and freedom of expression and religion. My desire to see an America that values all religious traditions encourages me to learn about what my neighbor next door believes. I want people of other faiths to experience the joy I have felt worshiping freely in this country. My deepest hope is that America will set the example for the world of the peaceful coexistence of different religious traditions within one nation.

Finally, I work for peaceful cooperation between different groups because my religious understanding of Jesus commands me to love my neighbor. I try as best I can to take that rule at face value without placing qualifications on it. Jesus did not say to only love one kind of person with one kind of belief. Jesus tells me to love everyone. And as a Christian minister, I follow that rule as best I can by loving my neighbors, even—maybe especially—those who believe in different ways of following God and those who don't believe in God at all. They are all people, and they are all my neighbors. Ultimately, learning about other religions only makes me love my own faith more. My hope for each of you reading this book is that you will grow in your tradition, while I continue to grow in mine.

One final note about the questions and answers that are the backbone of this book. The majority of the questions that come to me are from Christians, so naturally I answer them out of our mutual Christian tradition. When a person of another faith has sent me a question, I offer answers in consultation with clergy of that faith in the hopes of respecting their tradition. I have been honored by the thousands of e-mails that have come to me from around the world at *Beliefnet.com*, and I'm saddened that I can only answer a fraction of them. I pray that in these pages you will find many of your questions answered and through them find your own path to a full and enriching spiritual and religious life.

CHAPTER 1

BELIEF & FAITH

FAITHFACT ➤ Although the stereotype is that most teenagers are turned off by religion, the truth is that about two-thirds of American twelfth-graders do not feel alienated from organized religion.

Spiritual, not religious?

Dear Pastor Paul,

I have a good friend who plays with me on the tennis team. I invited him to youth fellowship at my church, but he told me that he was "spiritual, not religious." I have heard this before, but I don't really get it. What do you think the difference is between spiritual and religious?

Dear Friend,

"Spiritual, not religious" is a common phrase among people who may have a belief in God or a higher power; who see the

1

importance of meditation; or just feel the power of nature, but who don't see any benefits to organized religion. There is distrust on both sides of the spiritual versus religious issue. Religious people think those who call themselves spiritual are somehow false, weak or unable to commit to their beliefs. On the other hand, spiritual people are interested in a personal experience of *the spirit,* and they find that the rules, regulations and rituals of organized religion don't do anything for their own spiritual experience. They think that "Religion is what is left when the Spirit has left the building," as Bono has said.

My feeling is that religion and spirituality are better together than either one is alone. Religion can give you a community and a well-considered path to help you along your spiritual journey. However, if religion is lacking in individual spiritual experience, it can become just a habit and be empty of meaning.

So you can tell your friend, "I am spiritual *and* religious"—but only if that is true of you and your youth group.

CELEBRITY SPIRITUALITY

"I often wonder if religion is the enemy of God. It's almost like religion is what happens when the Spirit has left the building. God's Spirit moves through us and the world at a pace that can never be constricted by any one religious paradigm. I love that. You know, it says somewhere in the scriptures that the Spirit moves like a wind—no one knows where it's come from or where it's going. The Spirit is described in the Holy Scriptures as much more anarchic than any established religion credits. . . ."

Bono in the *Beliefnet* interview by Anthony DeCurtis

Why do I need religion?

Dear Pastor Paul,

I didn't grow up in any religion because my parents said they wanted us to decide for ourselves. Well, I'm now a junior in high school, and I still don't have any kind of faith or whatever. I am curious about religion, but I don't feel a real need for it in my life. So, why should I find a religion if I don't feel like I need one?

Dear Friend,

You should explore religion, even if only out of curiosity and a sense of adventure. New ideas are always worth looking at, and since most people in the world hold some kind of religious belief you'll understand how the majority of people around the world live and think. On a more personal level, religion offers a community of support, a clear moral guide for ethical behavior, and continues to be the chief source of human wisdom, passed on from generation to generation. Most importantly, religion provides clearly defined paths to what is sacred in the world and to God. Perhaps you're right that you don't need a religion, but the only way to find out is through personal investigation.

Religious **Traditions**

While it may seem like a contradiction, traditional religions are a great source for the spiritual seeker. Even if you're not planning on going through a formal initiation into a religion, learning about any faith can be a valuable part of your own search. Religions endure over time because they have provided answers for millions (even billions) of people. Religions offer their particular wisdom as the ultimate truth about the nature of life and the afterlife, answers about the existence of a higher power and how we might relate to that power, and guidelines for how to live our lives as individuals and as communities. Religions, in short, are interesting.

Investigate a religion with an open mind, and be prepared for it to inspire your own spiritual discipline.

Spiritual Activity #1
How about your friends?

Ask friends or acquaintances about their particular religious experience or belief. Steer them away from the "official line" on their religion. Instead, guide the conversation to their personal experience, which can be more informative and interesting and could even provide the basis for a stronger bond between you and your friends. Some examples of questions to ask are: How has your religion made your life better? How did you begin to follow your religion? Have there been any moments in your religious life that

really stand out? How does religion make you feel about yourself and about other people? What is your personal experience of God? You may wish to get five friends together and ask these questions of each other. Religion is very personal and important, so don't ridicule or judge each other. It is okay to disagree about matters of religion—just remember the golden rule of treating other people as you would like to be treated yourself.

Spiritual Activity #2
Check 'em out!

Investigate the rituals of a religion that interests you. Find out how often they worship and what participants are feeling when they go through their prayer or meditation. Learn how their community is formed and strengthened by their common devotion. Examine your own life in light of this knowledge. How often are you praying or participating in a spiritual ritual? How do you feel while you are engaged in religious devotion and afterward?

Spiritual Activity #3
What do they believe?

Research how different religions approach spirituality. Each religion has answers to the ultimate questions of life. You will gain wisdom by asking specific questions of any given religious tradition. Some examples of questions are: What does this religion believe about the existence of God or a higher power? What are human obligations in relation to this higher power? What are the creation stories of this religion that explain the makeup of the universe? What is the ultimate goal for each person within this religion? (Look at chapter 12 for an overview of the five largest world religions.)

How can I find the religion that is right for me?

Dear Pastor Paul,

I was raised in two different churches, Baptist and Episcopalian. I've recently become interested in Judaism, Hinduism and Buddhism, among other faiths. I believe in some of what each teaches but not all, so I find myself floating back and forth, looking for the day when I latch onto and completely believe in something. I'm so confused about what I should be doing and finding the right religion for me.

Dear Friend,
Some religious leaders complain of "cafeteria-style" faith—taking what we like from one religion and leaving the rest.

Personally, this approach doesn't bother me too much because I, like you, believe that all religions are valid and can help us to live good and spiritually fulfilling lives. While I am grateful to have gained so much wisdom from faiths other than my own, I am clear about the central importance of my own Christian faith and promote the value of going deeply into one religion.

I don't see a problem with where you find yourself right now. You are still young, and I expect that as you continue your search you will find the right religious community for you. You may wish to investigate the Unitarian Universalist tradition. Belief in the validity of all the world religions is an integral feature of their faith.

CELEBRITY SPIRITUALITY

Q: Do you consider yourself a religious seeker?

"Absolutely. I've tried to connect in every way that I can, whether it's spending time with various rabbis or speaking to groups like Hillel. And I've been reading to try to understand just what my Bar Mitzvah was all about. In a sense, all I did as a kid was memorize stuff. So I told my nephew at his Bar Mitzvah, 'Definitely look at this as something serious and learn from it. Make it a springboard for religious growth.' But as far as I was concerned as a kid, religion was drudgery, like having to go to more school. That attitude doesn't work for me anymore.

"Basically, I want to be as knowledgeable and grow as much as I can in every way possible. And the most important thing in life is religion, obviously. Now, I'm not going to sit here and pound the Torah for you! I just think it's important for everyone to know who they are."

WWF wrestler Bill Goldberg in the *Beliefnet* interview by John Spalding

Why I'm Unitarian Universalist

by Jonathan Ladd

"I've found you!" Emily exclaimed when she found our table at the student activities fair. Emily, a college freshman, had loved her high school youth group in Minnesota and was as happy to see us as we were to see her. In that moment Emily expressed the excitement so many of us feel about Unitarian Universalism.

I remember the first time I attended a meeting of our campus group. It was a time when I was feeling lonely. I felt like I didn't have a community of friends who would listen to me. What struck me immediately when I stepped through the door was how everyone was welcomed and loved no matter what. I didn't have to worry about acting right or saying a dumb thing. This place would always be a home for me as long as I wanted it to be.

As I kept coming back, I eventually learned that the welcoming spirit of Unitarian Universalism is not an accident, but a deeply rooted part of our proudly liberal religious heritage. The foundation of our UU faith is the acceptance of all people, no matter what we believe about God and the universe, no matter if we are gay or straight, black or white, rich or poor. This means a lot to me because it means that my UU faith can grow with me throughout my life, no matter where my experience and consciousness take me.

JUST THE FAQs
UNITARIAN
UNIVERSALISM

- A person who practices the Unitarian Universalist faith is Unitarian Universalist or "UU."

- Unitarian Universalism was originally a Christian faith but now acknowledges other religious founders in addition to Jesus.

- Unitarian Universalists worship in churches.

- Unitarian Universalist religious leaders are called ministers.

- Unitarian Universalists draw upon a wide range of texts they consider sacred including the Bible, Buddhist scriptures and poetry.

- Age: Unitarianism, 425 years; Universalism, 225 years; these two movements have been officially joined for 45 years.

- Country of origin: Transylvania (modern-day Romania) and United States.

- Number of American UUs: 650,000

- Number of UUs worldwide: 800,000

The best part of being a UU is when I go to my college UU group or visit another college or high school UU group. For so many of us, this is the only time all week we don't have to worry about dressing differently or acting cool. As I look around at these groups, I see people in preppy button-down shirts next to people with tattoos and purple hair, people who love theater next to people who love playing sports next to people who love cheerleading, people who know they're gay next to people who know they're straight and some others who just don't know yet, and on and on. . . . It is at these moments that I am most proud to be a Unitarian Universalist.

The way Unitarian Universalism has changed me most is in helping me see and appreciate the divine in every human soul. At its core, ours is a religion based on completely unconditional love. I'm so glad I found it!

 **FAITHFACT** 73% of college students in the USA have had a spiritual experience while in nature.

Can I worship outside instead of in church?

Dear Pastor Paul,

I am beginning to feel really uncomfortable in church. I'm bored, and I don't like the people. The place where I have felt closest to God was during a camping trip I took with some friends last year. I remember watching the sunrise and thinking about how beautiful the world is and thanking God for making it. My question is: Do I have to go to church to follow God?

Dear Friend,

I am so glad to hear about your experience out in nature. Being with God's creation in all its beauty, majesty and complexity can remind us that each of us is an important part of God's creation. It is wonderful to be alone in the wilderness from time to time—to think and pray and just be still. Ultimately, however, following God is not a completely solitary affair. God made humans to be in community with other human beings. In your search for God in nature, make sure you don't leave behind a whole group of God's creation—people. Church is not about buildings, it is about a community of people seeking and loving God. I hope you can find, or form, a community that shares your love of the outdoors with your love of God.

NATURE

I AM THE DUST IN THE SUNLIGHT, I AM THE BALL OF THE SUN . . .
I AM THE MIST OF MORNING, THE BREATH OF EVENING . . .
I AM THE SPARK IN THE STONE, THE GLEAM OF GOLD IN THE METAL . . .
THE ROSE AND THE NIGHTINGALE DRUNK WITH ITS FRAGRANCE.

I AM THE CHAIN OF BEING, THE CIRCLE OF THE SPHERES,
THE SCALE OF CREATION, THE RISE AND THE FALL.
I AM WHAT IS AND IS NOT . . .
I AM THE SOUL IN ALL.

Rumi, Sufi poet

Nature

A 2002 UCLA study showed that 72 percent of college students said they had experienced spirituality in nature in the past year—more than any other place. This is no surprise. Nature gives us a sense of awe at the beauty, intricacy and power of this world. The natural world inspires and humbles us, forcing (allowing) us to remember we are not the center of the universe, but part of a wider whole. It's significant that the Buddha, Jesus and Muhammad each experienced illumination in nature: under a Bodhi tree, in the wilderness and on a mountain. Fortunately, we all have access to nature. Even if you don't live out in the country you probably have several parks in your city that you could visit on a regular basis to uncover some of nature's spirituality.

Spiritual Activity #1
Getting to know nature . . .

Identify a tree or plant near your house you find particularly attractive. Really look at it, smell it and feel it. Take note of its color and design—learn its name as well as the insects or birds that make it their home. Follow the life of the plant throughout the year. Depending on the kind of plant and the area of the country you live in, the plant will undergo various changes with the seasons. The book of Ecclesiastes in the Hebrew scriptures declares, "To everything there is a season." Take note of the changes in the plant in winter, spring, summer and fall.

Nature can offer lessons about the cyclical nature of life. What wisdom can you gain from paying attention to the plant?

Spiritual Activity #2
Get connected to the whole . . .

Two important Buddhist concepts are compassion and interconnection. There is a saying that the flutter of a butterfly wing in Africa can affect the weather patterns in America. Each small thing we do is connected to every other event. For one day, act as if everything you do is hugely important. Consider every word, every action and every attitude as an important ingredient in the overall well-being of the world. See what changes—both within you and around you—as you maintain focus and attention to the details of your life.

Spiritual Activity #3
Do good for planet Earth.

Commit yourself to taking care of the natural world. Take part in an Earth Day celebration, work for a conservation group or just pick up trash in a local park. There is a Native American belief that we must be conscious of the effect our actions will have on the six generations coming after us. We care for those things we love, and in the act of loving and caring for the Earth, you will connect to the spirituality that nature inspires.

WHAT KIND OF SPIRITUAL PERSON ARE YOU?

Circle or write down the letter in front of the response that most closely corresponds to your belief.

1. I usually envision God as:

A. A personal being who loves us but also judges us
L. A spirit of love
F. A creative force or an energy that pervades through the world
D. I'm not sure he/she exists
B. I don't believe in God, but there is a higher spiritual dimension to life
X. I don't believe in God; what you see here is what you get.
W. Helping hands

2. I feel most spiritual when I am:

F. Out in nature, or in the act of making art
L. Having a deep conversation with my friends or a boyfriend/girlfriend
A. At a religious event, like a prayer service or Christian rock concert
W. Helping someone
X. I don't believe in the spiritual world
B. Practicing meditation
D. I don't really ever feel spiritual

3. My spiritual beliefs are important in my life because:

B. They provide the framework for my life and the way I progress along the spiritual path
A. They connect me to God's purpose for my life
D. Spiritual beliefs are not really that important to me
L. They give me a feeling of calm and strength, and console me when bad things happen
W. They make me treat people, and the world, better
F. They broaden my view of the mystery of the world
X. I have beliefs, but they're not spiritual

4. I most often talk to God:

L. In informal prayers that are like conversations
F. Through music or art
B. I connect to my own spirituality through meditation and other practices
X. What God?
D. I don't talk to God unless my parents tell me to pray
A. In prayers of thanks and petition
W. When I am talking to someone in need, as that is a symbol of God for me

5. If I had to pick one, I'd say my purpose in life is to:

W. Help to make the world a better place
L. Be a good friend/family member
F. Create something worthwhile
A. Obey God
D. I don't know what my purpose is
X. Accomplish something that will be my personal legacy
B. Live skillfully and dutifully

6. When I hear about bad things like child abuse or natural disasters, I think:

A. It's part of a plan—God will make it work for good
L. There must be some reason I don't understand now
B. Suffering exists in the world, but we do not have to remain in the suffering
X. Life sucks sometimes, but God has nothing to do with it one way or the other.
D. I don't know what to think
W. Whatever the bad thing is, my job is to make it better

7. People would treat others better if they:

- A. Followed God's law and the beliefs of my religion
- W. Followed the Golden Rule
- B. Understood that what goes around comes around
- X. People will keep doing what they do; it's a dog-eat-dog world
- L. Really got to know other people
- D. I don't know how people could treat each other better
- F. Found the source of inspiration and creativity in their lives and expressed it

8. When someone my age asks me what religion I am, I usually tell them:

- A. The beliefs of my religion, how it has changed my life and why it could help them too
- D. The faith I was raised in, but only because I don't know what else to say
- F. The spiritual path I am exploring now
- W. That what I believe is less important than how I live out my beliefs
- X. I think for myself and don't rely on a religion
- B. The nature of my beliefs

9. People at my school who have very different beliefs from me:

- F. Are just doing their own thing; live and let live
- D. Are okay, but sometimes seem a little weird
- A. Are on the wrong path and will be held accountable for it
- W. Are fine as long as I can see that they are helping other people
- L. Are really interesting, and I like connecting with them and learning from them
- B. Are entitled to and responsible for their own beliefs

10. The devil:

- X. Is just made up to scare people
- W. Is money and greed
- A. Is a real being who is dedicated to making horrible trouble in human affairs
- F. Is a symbol for bad things in the world
- B. Is not part of my belief
- L. Is a symbol for hate and fear that separates people

11. Going to religious or spiritual services is usually:

- L. Cool when I get to be with my friends at youth group
- A. One of the most important things I do during the week
- W. Less important than things like serving the hungry or housing the homeless
- X. Ridiculous
- D. Boring—I only go when my parents make me
- B. Helpful but not ultimately important
- F. Okay, but generally it is too routine and not creative enough

12. When I remember loved ones who have died, I think:

- A. I'll see them again in heaven
- L. I sense a spiritual connection to them, but I don't know what it is exactly
- X. They're just gone
- B. They are a part of the circle of life
- W. Of all the good they did in the world during their life
- D. I miss them, but I don't like to think about it

13. If I had to pick one, I'd say my beliefs or spiritual practices make me:

- W. Kinder—I treat people better
- B. More calm and balanced
- D. Confused
- A. The whole person that I am
- F. More inspired
- X. I don't have spiritual beliefs
- L. Closer to my family and friends

14. When I read a religious book or sacred text:

- A. My religious text offers the rules by which I live my life
- F. I look at it as literature and find it inspiring
- D. I'm bored stiff
- X. Why would I do that?
- B. True knowledge comes from within
- W. I look for guidelines on how to help others
- L. I am not as interested in books as I am in people

THE SCORING SYSTEM

Every person is different, and no quiz can tell you exactly what you're like. However, by looking at the first two letters that cropped up most often, you may be able to understand more about your spiritual life.

If you answered "A" a lot, you're secure in your religion, which may be the one you grew up in. You probably enjoy books, rituals, music and other things associated with your religion. To you, faith is positive, not restrictive. What to watch yourself for: Depending on how you express your faith—and where your friends are in their spiritual lives—your friends may admire your certainty or be put off by it. Don't change who you are to please anyone, but try not to come off as superior or too rigid.

If you answered "D" a lot, you're not all that interested in formal religion. Talk about spirituality may make you feel uncomfortable, and you'd rather not think about it. What to watch yourself for: It's fine to get some distance and take your time with the Big Questions, but keep in mind that you'll probably have to make a decision about what you believe someday.

If you answered "W" a lot, you're into action, not words. You may be very religious or not at all religious, but wherever you are, you feel strongly about helping others, especially the less fortunate. You probably measure people's spirituality by how much good they do. What to watch yourself for: Just remember that not everyone is as active as you or focused on results. Sometimes religion and spirituality are beneficial by themselves. Make sure you include some time for spiritual reflection to give you the energy and stamina for your work of changing the world.

If you answered "X" a lot, you may feel that religion is something made up to control people or let them keep their illusions. Being real—and realistic—is important to you, even if it means facing up to unpleasant facts. You probably find religious people annoying at best, and fake at worst. What to watch yourself for: Just remember that, even if you don't share their beliefs, religious people aren't stupid and deluded, they merely have a different worldview. Be respectful, even if you don't believe what religious people are saying.

If you answered "F" a lot, personal freedom and creativity are very important to you. You're not interested in labels or judging. Art and music are the ways that you best connect to the sacred. What to watch yourself for: Remember that other people find value in structure and traditions, even if they're not for you. Investigate the history of religious art and music as one way of connecting with the deep traditions in various religions.

If you answered "L" a lot, you're all about the love. Personal relationships and emotions are more important to you than almost anything else. You're into religion or spiritual practices as long as they address your feelings. What to watch yourself for: If religions focus too much on rules or behavior, you may drift off. Just remember to give your mind some attention, as well as your heart. And don't be afraid of time alone for reflection.

If you answered "B" a lot, you could be "spiritual but not religious," or you may be practicing Buddhism or Hinduism. The concept of a personal God doesn't interest you, but you are dedicated to your spiritual development. What to watch yourself for: Teachers are very important for helping people like you proceed on a good spiritual path. Choose your teachers wisely.

CHAPTER 2

TRADITIONS

FAITHFACT ⟩ 77% of college students in the USA believe that we are all spiritual beings.

Do I have to be baptized to enter heaven?

Dear Pastor Paul,
   I have never been baptized. Is baptism required to enter heaven?

Dear Friend,
   If you are a practicing Christian you should start the process of getting baptized—it is a truly a beautiful experience. The ritual of preparation will help you to grow in your faith. However, I am

a Universalist when it comes to the question of baptism. I feel that regardless of religious tradition, people who are loving and compassionate and serve the poor and love God as they understand God will go to heaven even if they are not baptized.

What The Religions Say About RITES OF PASSAGE

Buddhism

In many Asian countries and increasingly here in America, young men (and sometimes young women) perform a rite of passage during adolescence: The young person becomes a monk for three months, shaving his or her head, wearing monk's robes and living a monastic life. This rite is typically not for all Buddhists, but for those who are considering becoming a monk or a nun. In America there are centers that offer Buddhist rites of passage for young people, such as the program at the Tibetan Buddhist Shambhala Center in Boulder, Colorado, which introduces children to the contemplative arts and meditation.

Christianity

Most Christian denominations have a rite of passage called confirmation that introduces young people as members of the Christian community. The confirmation process consists of a series of classes on what it means to be an adult Christian and culminates in a ceremony in the church with young people confirming their infant baptisms and proclaiming their desire to become full members of the church. Baptist churches do not practice infant baptism; instead, a young person between the ages of twelve and fifteen will, of their own free will, decide to be a Christian and undergo the ritual of baptism by publicly declaring his or her faith and being immersed in a pool of water.

Hinduism

The eight major sacraments by which Hindu males of the Brahman caste progress through life are called *samskaras*. The specific rite that marks the passage from childhood to student is called *upanayana*, also known as the sacred thread ceremony. *Upanayana* essentially means to lead a child to the guru, and this rite of passage emphasizes that the young person is ready to begin the learning phase of life, especially as it relates to understanding the sacred Vedic scriptures. This ceremony can take place as early as age eight or as late as sixteen.

During the ceremony, a Hindu child receives three strands of three threads (nine threads in all) from his guru and places them over the right shoulder and under the left arm. He will wear the sacred threads for his entire life (changing them when they wear out). The child will then say the sacred Gayatri mantra. At the end of the ceremony the young person is considered "twice born."

There are also initiations for young women who receive the guru mantra and are initiated by a guru who will help them to grow spiritually.

Islam

There is no official rite of passage for young Muslims. Muslims are considered such at birth and do not undergo a specific ritual to achieve adult status. However, some Muslims view memorizing parts of the Qur'an or reading from the Qur'an in front of the *umma*, or community, as an unofficial rite of passage.

Judaism

The Bar Mitzvah or Bat Mitzvah happens when a Jewish boy turns thirteen or a girl turns twelve (though many girls celebrate at thirteen). At this age the young person becomes responsible for his or her own actions before God and the Jewish community. "Bar Mitzvah" means "son of the commandment," and "Bat Mitzvah" means "daughter of the commandment."

The occasion is marked by a Jewish boy or girl being called to read from the Torah for the first time. In Orthodox congregations, women do not read from the Torah, so girls mark their Bat Mitzvah in other ways—usually with a speech explaining the week's Torah portion, or by reading the Torah in a separate women's prayer service. After the reading, the young person will often make a short speech about the significance of becoming an adult within the Jewish community.

Are there any Christian vegetarians?

Dear Pastor Paul,

Are there any Christian vegetarians? This is to settle a disagreement, so it doesn't matter whether the person is in the Bible, or just a leader in the Christian faith, as long as he or she is vegetarian.

Dear Friend,

Yes, there are absolutely Christian vegetarians. While vegetarianism is not a requirement, many Christians practice vegetarianism and believe that basic Christian tenets of mercy and good stewardship of the Earth point toward it. (I even try to do this myself.) Some notable vegetarians in the past have been Leo Tolstoy, author of *War and Peace*; John Wesley, founder of the Methodist Church; Ellen White, founder of the Seventh Day Adventists church; the musician Moby; and even the Presbyterian minister Fred Rogers, who played Mr. Rogers on public television.

What The Religions Say About VEGETARIANISM

Buddhism

The first of the five precepts is "Do not harm living beings, and to cherish all life," which includes nonhumans. Although cruelty to animals is discouraged in Buddhism, not all Buddhists are vegetarians. In fact, the Dalai Lama, perhaps the world's most famous Buddhist, is a meat eater. Many Buddhists do practice vegetarianism, though, as it is seen as a way to promote the Buddhist values of loving-kindness and nonviolence.

Christianity

There are many Christians whose faith in Jesus inspires them to be vegetarians; however, most Christians believe that God gave humans dominion over other living creatures—and many interpret this to mean that it's okay to kill animals for food. Many Christians do, however, think it's important to not treat animals with cruelty. Some Christians give up meat during the Lenten fast in the forty days before Easter.

Hinduism

Hindu tradition discourages eating beef, and therefore most Hindus are vegetarians. The cow is seen as a special animal and is not allowed to be slaughtered. The principle of *ahimsa*—not doing injury or causing pain to living beings, including animals—also factors into Hindu vegetarianism.

Islam

Islam requires certain dietary restrictions (called *halal*), but vegetarianism is not among them. Islam does see treating animals with respect and without cruelty as important, however, and many *hadith* (the sayings of the prophet Muhammad) relate to this idea.

Judaism

The Jewish dietary laws, known as kosher laws, advocate showing mercy to animals during slaughter, and kosher meat is produced in a way that is as painless to animals as possible. But Judaism does not go as far as promoting vegetarianism.

Is the rosary just
for Catholics?

Dear Pastor Paul,

I am a Christian, but I like the idea of praying the rosary. How can I adapt the rosary to fit Christianity, or are there prayers I can say? Is the rosary just for Catholics?

Dear Friend,

To digress for just a moment about labels: Protestants, Evangelicals, Catholics and Eastern Orthodox are all Christians, and represent important traditions within one faith. So to ask whether or not you can adapt the rosary to fit Christianity doesn't exactly make sense, as it is already an important part of Christian practice in the Catholic Church.

Praying the rosary involves saying a very particular set of prayers that refer to the life of Jesus and Mary, the mother of Jesus. These prayers are of Catholic tradition, and revere Mary as the mother of God more deeply than Protestant Christian traditions. So you may not feel comfortable saying the rosary. However, if your interest is in the prayer beads themselves, you should know that other faiths, such as Islam and Buddhism, use a chain of beads as a way of focusing prayer. You may wish to pray with beads and say the Lord's Prayer with each bead, or use the beads as a way of counting the blessings in your life. In this way prayer beads are absolutely available to you.

Why I'm Orthodox Christian

by Virginia Pourakis

Sometimes tears just flow from my eyes. Most often it happens in church during the Divine Liturgy—I'll just be standing there or singing certain hymns in the choir or approaching the chalice for Holy Communion, and it will happen. But it can also happen whenever I witness or hear or feel something that touches and moves me so deeply, something that reveals to me but a speck of the awesome mystery that is the Lord our God—his love, his creations, his Son, his divine grace and the Holy Spirit. So it might happen when I'm listening to beautiful music, or when I am in the presence of a holy monk, or when I see little children interacting, or when I feel truly repentant during the confession of my sins before God, face-to-face with a priest, or when I am standing before an icon of the Virgin Mary that had earlier wept miraculous tears of holy oil, or when I witness a friend's sorrow, piety, humility or inner peace. I can't describe it as crying really, because when it happens the rest of my body is silent and still. So when it happens, usually no one notices, just me. And it is like my little secret, a joyful secret between God and me.

Some people call Orthodoxy itself "the best-kept secret in America." Yes, many people know very little about it, but in this sense it is a hidden treasure. That is one of the reasons I think it is so special. It is a deep and holy religion, and those

JUST THE FAQs ORTHODOX CHRISTIANITY

- Orthodox Christians are a branch of Christianity, often referred to by their country of origin. For example: Greek Orthodox or Russian Orthodox. "Coptic" is the word for the Orthodox Church in Egypt.

- The founder of the faith is Jesus Christ.

- Orthodox Christians worship in churches.

- Orthodox Christian religious leaders are called priest, father and presbyter.

- The Orthodox sacred text is the Bible.

- Age: 2,000 years

- Country of origin: Israel/Palestine; Constantinople (modern-day Istanbul)

- Number of Orthodox Christians worldwide: 150 million

- Number of Orthodox Christians in America: 2 million

- Time in USA: 220 years

who discover what it is all about—whether they are Orthodox or not—are often very inspired.

I am the way I am because of my Eastern Orthodox Christian faith. That is no secret to me. It truly is the core and fabric of my being. I cannot remember a time when it did not affect my everyday life, especially since I was confirmed (chrismated) as an infant at my baptism (where I also had my first communion). My faith provides me with guidelines for living and helps provide me with a healthy and balanced way of looking at the world. It teaches me to lead by example. It teaches me to be humble. And I have so much more to learn! For now, I especially love knowing that I am a member of the Christian church in one of its oldest forms, participating in an ancient form of worship, one that emphasizes deep reverence. It feels appropriate to me because I feel the truth was there from the beginning.

Am I going to church on the wrong day?

Dear Pastor Paul,

I am a nineteen-year-old student who goes to church on Sundays. My boyfriend is a Seventh Day Adventist, and he is always telling me that I am wrong for going to church on Sundays. I feel that as long as I am attending and believing it shouldn't matter on what day I go to church.

Dear Friend,

Different Christian traditions have their particular ways of worshiping and living out their faith. It is hard to say one is wrong, or better, than the other, as each tradition arose out of a particular context and need. Christians in the first centuries worshiped on Sundays to differentiate themselves from Jewish worship on Saturdays. Your boyfriend's religion, founded in the 1840s, has decided to follow the rule of Sabbath as understood in the Hebrew scriptures (Old Testament).

You should feel free to adopt your boyfriend's beliefs if you want, but at the same time you may rest assured that your practice of going to church on Sunday is not in the least bit wrong.

How can I get my minister to meet with me?

Dear Pastor Paul,

I love church, and my pastor really hits home with his sermons! But he is *sooo* busy, he never has time to get to know me. I would love to pay him a call to discuss with him what he says in his sermons and what I read in the Bible. When I call and ask to have him visit, though, he never does. If I ask him, he says to call and set up an appointment, and they just say they will pass on my request! What do I do?

Dear Friend,

Your pastor has a moral obligation to meet and get to know the members of his church. He will likely be too busy to meet with you on a regular basis, however. He does have to prepare those home-run sermons, after all.

I would suggest writing him a letter, explaining how a specific sermon affected you and asking him to meet with you once so you can thank him in person. He and his office should respect that request. You might also form a group in your congregation that goes to lunch after the service to talk about the sermon you've all just heard and discuss how it applies to your lives. That way you will have a forum to discuss your thoughts and hopefully make some new friends.

FAITHFACT 27% of teenagers have contributed money to their religious organization.

Why are pastors always asking for money?

Dear Pastor Paul,

I would like to know why Baptist pastors are always asking for money. I am Muslim, and in my religion that is a very bad thing to do.

Dear Friend,

I've been told by a Muslim friend that collecting money at mosques and Islamic fundraising events is not prohibited, but is perhaps more of a private matter between the person and God. As you well know, Muslims are expected to give alms (*zakat*) as one of the five pillars of Islam.

A Christian is expected by tradition (although many of us fail) to give 10 percent of their money to the church. Most Baptist churches are functioning on their own, with no financial support from a larger church hierarchy such as exists in the Catholic Church. The only way to pay for the building, the staff and any mission work (feeding the hungry, housing the homeless) comes from donations by the members of the congregation.

If a pastor asks you for money, you can politely decline.

What The Religions Say About GIVING

Buddhism

Dana is translated from the Pali language as giving. Almsgiving is considered a way of cultivating selflessness, compassion and nonattachment. This includes giving money to monks, nuns and teachers, as well as the poor. Buddhism does not specify a certain amount.

Christianity

Many churches urge their members to follow the biblical exhortation to give 10 percent of one's income back to God. This number comes from Deuteronomy 14:22, which says: "Set apart a tithe (a tenth) of all the yield of your seed that is brought in yearly from the field." While some churches expect all of that to go to their church, others hope that people will divide that 10 percent between their church and other charities.

Hinduism

There is no official amount that Hindus are expected to give, but Hindus do pay for *pujas* (rituals) in the temple and donate money to support their temples, which are considered religious duties in Hinduism. Hindus also donate *daan* (alms) to holy men and the poor.

Islam

 Zakat, one of the five pillars of Islam, is the concept of giving to charity and to the religion. *Zakat* is Arabic for "purification" and "growth." Those who can afford to give consider it a monetary act of worship. Muslims may also choose to give voluntary charity, or *sadaqah*, on top of *zakat*.

Judaism

Tzedakah is Hebrew for righteousness as it applies to charity and social justice. Synagogues are supported by donations and membership dues, but Jews are expected to give to the poor on top of that. Ideally, 10 percent of a person's income is expected.

How long should I fast for?

Dear Pastor Paul,

I've been considering a period of fasting and praying. How long should I fast, and what kind of fast should I try?

Dear Friend,

Good for you for exploring ways to deepen your spiritual life. Fasting is a time-honored way to focus on the Spirit.

Just a couple of warnings about fasting: Don't let it become a public demonstration of how spiritual you can be. Jesus warns against this in Matthew 6:16–18. Also, don't let fasting become an obsession. Before he achieved enlightenment, the Buddha got heavily into fasting, to the point where he couldn't even lift himself up anymore. Ultimately, the Buddha decided that extreme fasting was not the path to enlightenment, rather a more balanced approach to spiritual life he called "the middle way." In addition to discussing fasting with your parents and your spiritual leader, make sure that your body can handle fasting. It's not for everyone. You may wish to check with your doctor to make sure that fasting is okay for you.

Fasting should be done in connection with other activities that nurture spiritual growth. As an introduction, start out with a one-day fast (water only) from sunup to sundown. Throughout the day, try various soul-enriching activities, such as centering prayer or meditation, walking in nature, writing in a journal, or performing some kind of service to your fellow humans. Have a simple, peaceful meal at night and reflect on your experience.

HOW MUCH DO YOU KNOW ABOUT RELIGIONS?

Circle or write down the letter in front of the response that most closely corresponds to your belief.

1. The campus Jewish organization Hillel is named after:

A. A mountain in Israel where sacred learning was passed down

B. A mystical writing dating back to the fifth century

C. An impoverished rabbi who was sometimes unable to pay the admission fee to study Torah

2. The most popular poet read in America today is:

A. The Hindu sage-poet Rabindranath Tagore

B. The thirteenth-century Sufi mystic Rumi

C. The Catholic poet Gerard Manley Hopkins

3. Which religious leader brought Hinduism to America via the 1893 World Parliament of Religions in Chicago?

A. Satguru Nehru

B. Mahatma Gandhi

C. Swami Vivekananda

4. Which is NOT true of Moses?

A. He had a speech impairment (perhaps a stutter)

B. He led the Israelites out of Egyptian slavery

C. He entered the Promised Land triumphantly

5. Khadija, the first wife of the Prophet Muhammad, was:

A. A successful businesswoman and caravan owner

B. A poor beggar woman who came to him for help

C. Several years younger than him

6. In the Bible, the apostle Paul underwent a Christian conversion when:

A. He saw a bright light and heard a voice saying, "Saul, why do you persecute me?"

B. The stones he was throwing at a martyr bounced off the martyr harmlessly

C. He eavesdropped on the Last Supper

7. In the Hebrew scriptures, what woman enters a royal beauty contest, becomes queen and saves her people?

A. Deborah

B. Esther

C. Rebecca

8. It's said that Lao-tzu wrote:

A. The Diamond Sutras (Buddhism)

B. The *Tao Te Ching* (Taoism)

C. The Qur'an (Islam)

9. The best-selling Christian Science text *Science and Health with Key to the Scriptures* was written by:

A. Joachim Fable

B. Mary Baker Eddy

C. Hildegard von Bingen

10. The town of Najaf, Iraq, contains a shrine to Ali, son-in-law of the Prophet Muhammad. It's therefore sacred to:

A. Sunni Muslims

B. Shiite Muslims

C. Santerians

11. To what early Christian leader did Jesus say "Feed my sheep"?

A. Peter
B. Paul
C. Phillippa

12. The Baha'i leader Baha'u'llah was:

A. The next crown prince of Persia who forsook his thrown
B. Illiterate
C. Exiled from his country

13. Which Catholic saint known as the "Little Flower" became a Doctor of the Church (officially recognized theological writer)?

A. Therese of Lisieux
B. Teresa of Avila
C. Francis of Assisi

14. The patriarch considered by Jews to be the founder of the Hebrew people through his son Isaac, and by Muslims to be the founder of the Arab peoples through his son Ishmael, was:

A. Noah
B. David
C. Abraham

15. Which religious figure was said to have been sitting under a tree when he gained enlightenment?

A. Buddha
B. Pope Leo
C. Confucius

16. Martin Luther is to Martin Luther King Jr. as:

A. Calvinist organ player is to Church of Christ preacher

B. Protestant reformer is to Baptist minister
C. Medieval Catholic saint is to Presbyterian minister

17. What is the name of the religious leader who discovered golden tablets engraved with sacred writings that became the Book of Mormon?

A. Joseph Smith
B. John Smith
C. William Johnson

18. Which twentieth-century British author worked on the *Book of Shadows*, wrote *Witchcraft Today* and is considered the founder of modern Wicca?

A. Gerald Gardner
B. Starhawk Ravenwolf
C. Sir Henry Mimsy

19. Charles Wesley, the brother of Methodist leader John Wesley, is known for his:

A. Popular church hymns
B. Praise guitar music
C. Eclectic Hindu-Christian chants

20. According to the gospels, the first person the resurrected Jesus appeared to was:

A. His mother Mary
B. The beloved disciple John
C. Mary Magdalene

21. The Hindu God, Lord Ganesha, is invoked because of his power to:

A. Overpower enemies in battle
B. Help attract a possible love interest
C. Remove obstacles in the way of success

1. C 3. C 5. A 7. B 9. B 11. A 13. A 15. A 17. A 19. A 21. C
2. B 4. C 6. A 8. B 10. B 12. C 14. C 16. B 18. A 20. C

FAMILY

Can I be my family's religion— but on my own terms?

Dear Pastor Paul,

I was born in Vietnam and, like many South Asians, my family is Buddhist. My parents are devout and strongly encourage me to follow that path. I don't really want to because I strongly disagree with the strong emphasis that Buddhism places on family values rather than individualism. Is that true? What is the basis for Buddhist values?

Dear Friend,

It sounds like you want to practice the same religion as your parents—but on your own terms. You feel your parents' Buddhism stifles your individuality, and they use it to support their strong belief in obedience to the family. This doesn't make them bad Buddhists or bad parents, it's simply the tradition they know and practice. However, it may not be right for you.

Oftentimes, people look for truths in other religions when their truth may well be found in their own religion. It's great to hear you asking deeper questions about Buddhism.

While the Buddha did teach that everyone owes a great debt to their parents, his teachings focused almost entirely on the individual and his or her own path to enlightenment. Buddhism teaches that each of us has sole responsibility for cultivating our own mindfulness, wisdom and compassion. The emphasis your parents place on family responsibility is probably due more to their Asian heritage than to actual Buddhist teachings.

While it's important to respect the tradition your parents practice, I hope you'll continue to explore Buddhism on your own terms. Check out some writings of contemporary Buddhist teachers, or visit a temple or practice center of your choosing. Remember, traditions are only as alive as each new generation makes them.

Can I talk to my grandmother about religion even if we disagree?

Dear Pastor Paul,

I do not believe in the traditional God, with the judgment and all that comes with it. But my grandmother is a devout Catholic and cannot be persuaded any which way against "the Good Book." My question is this: Should I share my feelings with my grandmother or keep them to myself?

Dear Friend,

If you have a good relationship with your grandmother, you should share your beliefs with her and listen to her beliefs. You and she may never really agree, but be respectful and you may find out incredible things about her life. Ask her when God has most been present in her life. Ask her how she would describe God. Ask her how she experiences God in day-to-day life. Stay away from the Bible if that is a trouble spot and instead learn about the wonders and difficulties of your grandmother's life and how God has been there for her. Along with deeper under-standing of God, you may find your relationship with your grandmother growing as well.

Will my dog go to heaven?

Dear Pastor Paul,

My dog just died that I have had since I was four, and I am really sad and miss her so much. I know this is going to sound insane, but is it possible that she will go to heaven and I will see her there? My friends say that only humans go to heaven, but I don't know one way or another.

Dear Friend,

Anyone who has had a pet knows that animals are not merely machines, but have strong personalities (for lack of a better word) and spirits all their own. Many churches recognize the place animals have in our lives by inviting people to bring their pets for a blessing during the feast of St. Francis.

I believe that animal spirits live on after death. God created all living beings, and my guess is that heaven is not an exclusive club just for humans, but that all of God's creatures will be there.

PRAYER FOR ANIMALS

GOD OUR HEAVENLY FATHER, YOU CREATED THE WORLD TO
SERVE HUMANITY'S NEEDS AND TO LEAD THEM TO YOU.
BY OUR OWN FAULT WE HAVE LOST THE BEAUTIFUL RELATIONSHIP
WHICH WE ONCE HAD WITH ALL YOUR CREATION.
HELP US TO SEE THAT BY RESTORING OUR RELATIONSHIP
WITH YOU WE WILL ALSO RESTORE IT WITH ALL YOUR CREATION.
GIVE US THE GRACE TO SEE ALL ANIMALS AS GIFTS FROM YOU
AND TO TREAT THEM WITH RESPECT, FOR THEY ARE YOUR CREATION.
WE PRAY FOR ALL ANIMALS WHO ARE SUFFERING
AS A RESULT OF OUR NEGLECT. MAY THE ORDER YOU ORIGINALLY
ESTABLISHED BE ONCE AGAIN RESTORED TO THE WHOLE WORLD
THROUGH THE INTERCESSION OF THE GLORIOUS VIRGIN MARY,
THE PRAYERS OF ST. FRANCIS AND THE MERITS OF YOUR SON,
OUR LORD JESUS CHRIST WHO LIVES AND REIGNS
WITH YOU NOW AND FOREVER. AMEN.

Saint Francis of Assisi

 **FAITHFACT** Regular religious service attendance, high personal importance on faith and many years spent participating in religious youth groups are clearly associated with safer, healthier, more constructive lifestyles for U.S. teenagers.

Should parents force their kid into going to church?

Dear Pastor Paul,

Do you think it's right for a parent to force their kids into going to church?

Dear Friend,

This is going to make me unpopular, but I believe it's okay for parents to require their kids to go to church until they move out on their own. Just like going to school or doing basic chores, going to church is something your parents are within their rights to ask. If the whole family goes, you should go. In hindsight, I am glad that my parents forced me to go to church, even when I was not always exactly enthusiastic.

That doesn't mean you shouldn't engage your parents in a real conversation about belief and church. Ask them why it is important to them that you attend, and really listen to their reasons. Then, in a nonconfrontational manner, tell them your thoughts about faith and church and why you don't like to go. Try to do this at a time other than Sunday morning when you are tired and irritable. It may not change their minds, but it may help you to understand one another better. And one day, in about twenty-five years, you may thank them.

FAMILY

THY LORD HAS DECREED . . .
THAT YOU BE KIND TO PARENTS. WHETHER ONE OR
BOTH OF THEM ATTAIN OLD AGE IN YOUR LIFETIME, DO NOT SAY
TO THEM A WORD OF CONTEMPT, NOR REPEL THEM,
BUT ADDRESS THEM IN TERMS OF HONOR. AND, OUT OF KINDNESS,
LOWER TO THEM THE WING OF HUMILITY AND SAY,
"MY LORD! BESTOW ON THEM THY MERCY EVEN AS
THEY CHERISHED ME IN CHILDHOOD."

Qur'an 17.23

A BABY IS GOD'S OPINION THAT THE WORLD
SHOULD GO ON.

Carl Sandburg

TO PUT THE WORLD RIGHT IN ORDER, WE MUST FIRST
PUT THE NATION IN ORDER; TO PUT THE NATION IN ORDER,
WE MUST FIRST PUT THE FAMILY IN ORDER; TO PUT THE
FAMILY IN ORDER, WE MUST FIRST CULTIVATE OUR PERSONAL LIFE;
WE MUST FIRST SET OUR HEARTS RIGHT.

Confucius

SUPPORTING ONE'S FATHER AND MOTHER,
CHERISHING WIFE AND CHILDREN AND A PEACEFUL OCCUPATION;
THIS IS THE GREATEST BLESSING.

Buddhism

IF YOU AS PARENTS CUT CORNERS,
YOUR CHILDREN WILL TOO. IF YOU LIE, THEY WILL TOO.
IF YOU SPEND ALL YOUR MONEY ON YOURSELVES AND
TITHE NO PORTION OF IT FOR CHARITIES, COLLEGES, CHURCHES,
SYNAGOGUES AND CIVIC CAUSES, YOUR CHILDREN WON'T EITHER.
AND IF PARENTS SNICKER AT RACIAL AND GENDER JOKES,
ANOTHER GENERATION WILL PASS ON THE POISON ADULTS STILL
HAVE NOT HAD THE COURAGE TO SNUFF OUT.

Marian Wright Edelman

✦

DO NOT DESPISE THE BREATH OF YOUR FATHERS,
BUT DRAW IT INTO YOUR BODY.
THAT OUR ROADS MAY REACH TO WHERE THE LIFE-GIVING ROAD OF
OUR SUN FATHER COMES OUT,
THAT, CLASPING ONE ANOTHER TIGHT,
HOLDING ONE ANOTHER FAST,
WE MAY FINISH OUR ROADS TOGETHER;
THAT THIS MAY BE, I ADD TO YOUR BREATH NOW.
TO THIS END:
MAY MY FATHER BLESS YOU WITH LIFE;
MAY YOUR ROAD REACH TO DAWN LAKE,
MAY YOUR ROAD BE FULFILLED.

Zuni Prayer

✦

TRAIN UP A CHILD IN THE WAY THEY SHOULD GO,
AND WHEN THEY ARE OLD THEY WILL NOT DEPART FROM IT.

Proverbs 22:6

How can I understand my pagan sister?

Dear Pastor Paul,

My twin sister recently professed herself a pagan. I always knew she was different, but since we both moved away to college I've found her very difficult to understand. We were baptized, took first communion and were confirmed together, and these things have always meant so much to me. I feel like she has turned her back on me, as well as the church. We live together, and I want to play my CDs by Christian bands like Delirious and CJM really loud, but I don't want to hurt her feelings. What should I do?

Dear Friend,

It's obvious you love your sister and long for connection with her. That love is going to help you work through your differences. It also makes it okay to disagree strongly with what she believes. The two of you can still get along, and you can do so precisely by continuing to express yourselves. Ask your sister to explain her beliefs to you, and explain yours to her. And play your music—loud, and let her play her music loud. Both of you have a right to your religion and your music.

How can my parents be happy about my decision to be a nun?

Dearest Pastor Paul,

Praise be Jesus Christ! I'm seventeen years old and very close to the Lord! Jesus has become so real these past few years that I have finally made my decision: I am to become a Felician Franciscan Sister. But my parents aren't religious at all, and they don't understand what attracts me to God and the Blessed Sacrament. I don't know how or when to tell them. If you have any advice it would be greatly appreciated. May the peace of the Father, Son and Holy Spirit be with you always!

Dear Friend,

Congratulations! I'm glad that you have found your calling in life and have come to this monumental decision. You should finish high school, turn eighteen, and be ready to move out of the house before you make any official declarations. At that time you will be recognized as an adult and expected to make your own life decisions.

In addition to informing your parents of your decision in person, write them a letter explaining your experience of Jesus Christ and how it has transformed your life. Describe in detail why you feel called to a life as a Franciscan Sister and how you intend to use this life that God has given you. Sometimes it is hard for people to digest radically new information at one time, and having a letter to reference can help.

The most important thing is to show them that you will continue to be the loving daughter they have always known. Even if they resist at first, they'll come to be happy for you if they see how happy and fulfilled you are.

What The Religions Say About WOMEN

Buddhism

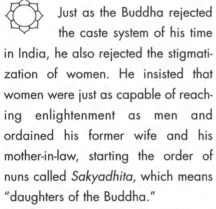 Just as the Buddha rejected the caste system of his time in India, he also rejected the stigmatization of women. He insisted that women were just as capable of reaching enlightenment as men and ordained his former wife and his mother-in-law, starting the order of nuns called *Sakyadhita*, which means "daughters of the Buddha."

After the Buddha's time, the status of women in many traditional Buddhist countries shifted. Today, women's current status depends on the culture of the particular country. In recent years, Buddhist countries have begun to allow the ordination of women again. Young women in America will find Buddhism quite egalitarian among the sexes. There are many women teachers who lead dharma centers and are available as mentors. There are also monasteries for young women who wish to study Buddhism more intensely.

Christianity

Women have always played an important role in Christianity. Jesus had many women among his followers. According to the Bible, it was the women who stayed with Jesus when others had abandoned him at his death on the cross. When he was resurrected, Jesus first appeared to three women. Catholics and Orthodox Christians have traditions of strong devotion to Mary, the mother of Jesus, to whom they pray daily.

That said, Christian leadership has historically been dominated by men. The Roman Catholic Church and the Orthodox Church continue to have exclusively male clergy. Many mainline Protestant churches do ordain women as ministers and priests. However, most of the more conservative Evangelical denominations, such as the Southern Baptists, welcome women as church leaders but forbid their ordination to clergy.

Hinduism

Although there is mention of women priests and leaders in the sacred Vedic texts, most Hindu priests today are men. In traditional Hinduism, women have generally filled supporting roles to their male counterparts. That said, the Hindu pantheon is full of female role models, including the strong and brave Goddess Durga, who rode on a lion and vanquished her foes; the fierce Goddess Kali, a manifestation of Durga, who wore a garland of skeletons around her neck; Sarasvati, the consort of Lord Brahma who is the Goddess of wisdom and learning;

and finally there is the Mother Goddess of all Hindu Gods, worshiped all over India as Devi.

In recent years, Hindu women in India and the United States have gained a great deal of political, social and increasingly religious power. Many American Hindus and people of other religions look up to female gurus like Ammachi, known as the Hugging Saint, for providing comfort and healing through her warm hugs.

Islam

While it is popular to criticize Islam as a faith that veils women and submits them to second-class citizenship, it is important not to generalize about the status of women in Islam. Historians have made clear that the plight of women in what is now known as Saudi Arabia was greatly improved by the arrival of the Prophet Muhammad and the establishment of Islamic law. Prior to the advent of Islam, female babies were often killed, women were treated like animals with no rights in marriage, and women were never included in any inheritance. Under Islam, women became entitled to inheritance, to keep all their earnings if they worked, and overall gained much more power and respect than they had before Islam. Islamic law declares women and men to be equal, and the rules and restrictions of the faith apply to both sexes.

In America's pluralistic society, young Muslim women have many options about how they wish to practice their faith. This includes choosing whether or not to wear the *hijab*, the traditional head covering. Many Muslim women wear *hijab* out of a desire to follow Islamic laws about modesty, finding these laws have personal relevance to them. Others choose not to wear *hijab* (except while in the mosque), and they are still widely respected within the Muslim community.

Judaism

While the founders of Judaism are commonly called "the patriarchs," women have always had an important place in the Jewish story. Judaism offers wonderful role models for women, including biblical figures like Esther, Ruth and Naomi, and Moses's sister Miriam. In traditional Judaism, women and men have different roles in the synagogue and in the home. The strictest differences between the sexes are found in Orthodox Judaism. Men and women pray in separate areas of the synagogue, and women are not permitted to lead prayer services or read from the Torah if men are present.

Conservative and Reform congregations, however, allow men and women to pray together, and women are allowed to read from the Torah. There have been major feminist advances in recent times, even within the Orthodox movement, leading to the growth of women's prayer groups and the celebration of Rosh Chodesh (the first day of every month) as a women's festival. Some Jewish women have even adopted rituals like placing a *cos Miriam*, or "Miriam's cup," on the seder table to honor the role of Miriam in the Passover story and to provide a female counterpart to the tradition of Elijah's cup. Jewish religion in America is very diverse, and young women from different paths of faith can find comfort within Jewish tradition. Young women who are looking to be ordained clergy in Judaism will probably attend a Reform, Reconstructionist or Conservative seminary, as these denominations ordain women rabbis.

CHAPTER 4

INTERFAITH DATING

Did God break us up?

Dear Pastor Paul,

My boyfriend recently broke up with me because he said God told him he had to. He told me he loves me too much, and it's sinful because his mind is always on me, instead of God. It's against the First Commandment, he says, because his love makes me his idol. He said he isn't ready for marriage, and that the right time to date is when a person is ready. I grew up learning Buddhist ideas. It baffles me that he could make such a decision. Can you help me understand where he is coming from?

Dear Friend,

The First Commandment requires that we love the Lord with all our heart. If your former boyfriend was so obsessed with you that he forgot to love God, then he's right—he's not mature enough to be dating. A real boyfriend is capable of loving you, his family, his friends, his neighbor and God all at the same time. Love doesn't have to have limits. I suggest you practice the Buddhist principle of nonattachment and try to be compassionate toward him while letting him go.

By the way, when people tell you they are doing something unpleasant because God told them to do it—watch out.

Can I go out with a non-Christian?

Dear Pastor Paul,
I like this girl who isn't a Christian. Is it right for me to go out with her?

Dear Friend,

I don't know if going out with the girl who is not Christian is right or wrong for you. But you might ask yourself: Does it bother you that she is not Christian? Do you want her to change? If the answer is yes, you should probably not go out with her unless you are clear with her and yourself that you are hoping for her conversion to your faith.

A person's religious conviction should be a part of how you pick a girlfriend or boyfriend. Would you pick a girl who did not have the kind of face you wanted in hopes that she would get plastic surgery? No, of course not. If, on the other hand, you admire the faith this girl does practice and think that it might enrich the Christian faith that you already hold, you should ask her out.

Dating a Buddhist (If you're not one)

Generally Buddhists do not insist on others believing what they believe. You may occasionally encounter some restrictions with Asian Buddhists, whose dating requirements are likely to be based more on cultural traditions than religious.

Dating a Christian (If you're not one)

Young Christians are such a diverse group that it is difficult to establish universal guidelines. Many Christians will not go out with non-Christians, or will require the non-Christians to attend their Christian community in hopes of conversion. At the same time, there are many Christians who are less strict about interfaith dating, and so it is necessary to decide on a case-by-case basis.

Dating a Hindu (If you're not one)

In India, the majority of Hindu marriages are arranged by the families with the young persons' consent. While this might seem very odd to Americans, the success rate of these marriages is much higher than marriages arranged by young people for themselves. In America, this practice is not as widespread but still occurs occasionally when family bonds are very strong in Indian culture. With that in mind, a non-Hindu should feel free to approach a Hindu person and ask them on a date or group outing. Like Buddhists from Asian countries, many of the feelings you encounter about interfaith dating in Hinduism may stem from cultural ties to India rather than religious custom.

Dating a Muslim (If you're not one)

Traditional Muslims don't "date" in the conventional sense of the word; instead, many rely on family introductions to find a match to marry. If Muslim teens are allowed to date, the parents often have a lot to say about who their children date, especially girls. If you are interested in a Muslim as a date, try to be included on outings with a group of people. Muslim families often obey a strict moral code, and you should be very respectful as far as physical intimacy goes; for some Muslim women it is even forbidden to shake hands with the opposite sex.

Dating a Jew (If you're not one)

 Attitudes vary within Judaism about interfaith dating. Many Jews are concerned about the dwindling of the Jewish community, since Jews make up such a small percentage of the American population. Parents often fear that if their children date and marry non-Jews, their grandchildren will not be raised in Jewish homes. Interfaith dating in Judaism depends on the family. If you ask a Jewish girl or boy out on a date and they say they can't, don't take it personally. They may have turned you down because of religious dating restrictions.

How can I convince my parents to let me go to my boyfriend's Reform synagogue?

Dear Pastor Paul,

I come from a pretty strict Orthodox Jewish home, but I'm dating a guy who's Reform. His parents invited me to go to their synagogue with them one Saturday morning. I want to go, but my parents won't let me. They don't want me praying in a congregation that has mixed seating. How can I convince them to let me go?

Dear Friend,

It is not going to be easy to convince your parents. Often disagreements between branches of the same religion are as strong as between different religions. This is the case between Orthodox Judaism and Reform Judaism.

You may try to appeal on the precept of accepting hospitality offered by your boyfriend's family. Hospitality is very important in the Jewish religion, and it may be one way for your parents to look at this a different way. Another idea is to promise to have a really good conversation with your parents after returning from the service to talk about how you experienced the Reform synagogue in contrast to your Orthodox one. Hopefully, your parents will take advantage of this opportunity to have an open and frank conversation with their teenage daughter—an all-too-rare occurrence during the teenage years.

If your parents ultimately say no, then honor their wishes while you are under their roof. Given their beliefs, you may also be grateful they are not forbidding you to date this boy.

Why I'm Jewish

by Joseph Aaron Skloot

Candlelight. A white tablecloth. Gleaming silverware. Overflowing dishes of food. Family and friends around a communal table. *Shabbat*, the Jewish Sabbath. Well, maybe.

In my family growing up, we did things a little differently.

Traditionally, Jews celebrate *Shabbat* at home, commemorating the seventh day of creation and God's rest. It is a day of rest and peace: Jews don't work, don't use electrical appliances, don't spend money, avoid routine and mundane tasks.

These are all beautiful traditions, but we celebrated *Shabbat* untraditionally. From an early age, my parents brought me to synagogue, where we attended Friday night services. During these services (called *Kabbalat Shabbat* in Hebrew) we "welcomed" the Sabbath with lively songs and special prayers. We connected with other members of our Jewish community and with God. We sat

- A person who follows the religion called Judaism is a Jew or Jewish (a person can also be born Jewish).

- Jews worship in a temple or synagogue.

- A Jewish religious leader or teacher is called Rabbi.

- The primary sacred writing is called the Torah.

- Age: 4,000 years

- Country of origin: Israel/Palestine

- Number of American Jews: 6 million

- Number of Jews worldwide: 15 million

- Major Branches: Orthodox, Reform, Conservative, Reconstruction

- Time in USA: 350 years

in the front pew of our synagogue's beautiful sanctuary, very close to the *bimah*, the raised platform from where our rabbis and cantor led the service. (Our cantor used to say that our family sang louder than any other family in the congregation!)

After services, when I was little, we often attended a congregational dinner where everyone ate together. As I got older, I started going out to dinner with a group of friends my age who were also regulars at Friday night services. These dinners were always fun. We'd talk about the important events in our lives, and more often than not our conversations would hinge on a Jewish issue or concern. We were students from different schools; we had diverse interests; yet we were committed to celebrating *Shabbat* (in our unique way) and to Judaism itself.

In some ways, my Friday night experience was very different from the "traditional" *Shabbat*, but in other ways it was very similar. In joining in prayer and in community every week, my family and our dinner group truly fulfilled the ultimate goals of *Shabbat*: We rested; we reflected on the week gone by; we thanked and praised God for the beauty of creation and the opportunity to live our lives. Our Friday night rituals made *Shabbat* distinctly different from the rest of the week, full of action and intensity.

At the close of *Shabbat*, Saturday evening, Jews practice a ritual called *havdalah*, meaning "separation." In one *havdalah* prayer, we thank God for "drawing a distinction" between the holy and the ordinary, between *Shabbat* and the workweek.

Shabbat itself is all about distinctions. We do things differently on *Shabbat*. We avoid our routine habits and engage in other special rituals, thereby separating and sanctifying the *Shabbat* day itself. In my family, while we may not have eaten elaborate dinners or avoided flipping light switches, *Shabbat* still felt special, holy and different from every other day of the week. With our own weekly rituals, we transformed the seventh day into a day of rest, community, prayer and peace.

Is it okay for my brother to date a Wiccan?

Dear Pastor Paul,

I am Catholic, and my brother is seeing a girl who is Wiccan. Can you tell me something about Wicca? All I've heard is that witches are involved, and, well, that's an ouch right there. Help!

Dear Friend,

You hear the word "Wicca" and your mind sees pointy hats, broomsticks and evil spells. It's hard to rid ourselves of stereotypical images, but just as Jews, Protestants, Muslims and even Catholics have been misrepresented, so have Wiccans.

Wicca is an earth-based religion—falling under the larger umbrella of paganism. Wiccans worship a Goddess and a God and revere nature. They believe in "magick" (spelled that way to differentiate it from stage magic), and some do cast "spells," but these practices shouldn't be confused with Satan (a Christian concept) or black magic. Wiccans believe that magick is a divine energy that exists in everything, and spells channel these energies to create positive change. They are not hexes and curses, as popularly depicted. Witches are those who practice magick and can come from any background, not just Wicca or paganism.

Find out who this girl is on the inside and don't base your opinions on a label. I'm sure your brother's girlfriend would be happy to introduce you to some of her beliefs.

Why I'm Wiccan

by Layla Holguin

My bare feet brace on smooth rock as I bend down and submerge my hand in a cold stream. The breeze ruffles my unbound hair and the rays of the afternoon sun paint the insides of my eyelids red. Divinity is here, now, and so am I.

Wicca is an affirming religion. We walk upon a Sacred Earth and take our truth from her cycles. Now it is hot and dry; now it is cold and dark. Now we are born; now we die. Yes, spring will come again. We will be reborn—this is a journey. Life is change; we celebrate it.

I came to Wicca at fifteen, quite by accident—a simple matter of turning around at the right moment on the school bus. A moment of knowing that I had found it, of recognizing my way—a moment of *yes* that would not be turned aside. This is my path—a game trail in the woods, often solitary, guided by my inner wisdom. It is my path primarily because, beyond all other things, I love the Earth. Her peaks, trees and creatures are all alive to me. To Wiccans the Earth is sacred; the Goddess is the Earth.

Every day, I am supported by a religion that honors the female as divine—that honors the cycles of birth and death—and that provides me with a rich cross-cultural spectrum of Goddess images that reflect my multifaceted spirit. I am supported by a spirituality that affirms my instinctual and intuitive nature, my ability to know my own truth, and to preside at my own rituals. I am empowered by the understanding that the world is more than physical and that therefore I can create magickally. As a magick-maker, I am active, self-confident and responsible in my spirituality. My rituals mark and facilitate my moments of change. I follow the long history of those who have sought knowledge of the meeting of the physical and otherworlds.

Wicca is dynamic, diverse and nonhierarchical. It imposes no rules from without, but grows from within myself, from my connection to nature, both seen and unseen. I have found the essence of Wicca in a fallen leaf that catches my eye and finds a home on my altar and in the community rituals I have attended that draw from our diverse collective experience to create a sacred space and time from which we emerge changed and unified.

JUST THE FAQs
WICCA

- A person who follows the religion called Wicca is called a Witch or Wiccan.

- Wiccans worship outdoors with Mother Nature, or often in private homes.

- A Wiccan religious leader or teacher is called a priestess or priest.

- There is no one sacred book, but some reference the Book of Shadows.

- Age: Modern practice dates from the 1940s although it references back thousands of years.

- Country of origin: Northern Europe, primarily in British Isles

- Number of American Wiccans: 350,000

- Number of Wiccans worldwide: Due to persecution, Wiccans are often unwilling to make their religious affiliation known.

- Time in USA: 45 years

I like this Hindu guy, but am I the right caste?

Hey Pastor Paul,

I like this boy at school, and he kinda likes me back. He's Hindu and I'm Episcopalian. I don't think he even can go out with me, and I don't know what to do. I don't think he can date outside his caste, but I'm too afraid to ask him in case he gets irritable about it. **PLEASE HELP!**

Dear Friend,

There is no single rule for all Hindus about dating. Depending on how his family feels, he may be able to date you, or he may not. My suggestion to you is to keep on being his friend and show him, in appropriate ways, that you like him. If he can date you, and wants to date you, then go out!

Talking about his caste may not be appropriate if you fear he'll get irritated about your asking about it. He may be defensive, or maybe he has been teased about it in the past. Whatever happens between the two of you, my suspicion is that the caste system does not apply to non-Indian people.

HINDU CASTES

CASTE, ORDER, CLASS—VARNA

WITHIN TRADITIONAL INDIAN SOCIETY THERE ARE FOUR CLASSES THAT DETERMINE A PERSON'S ROLE IN SOCIETY. THE ENGLISH WORD TO DESCRIBE THIS ORDER—"CASTE"—COMES FROM THE PORTUGUESE WORD "CASTA," MEANING "BREED," AND WAS APPLIED TO THIS SYSTEM.

THE FOUR VARNAS ARE:

PRIESTS—BRAHMINS

RULERS/WARRIORS—KSHATRIYAS

ARTISANS/TRADERS—VAISHYAS

SERVANTS/LABORERS/FARMERS—SHUDRAS

◆

UNTOUCHABLES—DALITS

UNTOUCHABLES WERE PEOPLE WHO WERE OUTSIDE OF THE ORDER BECAUSE THEY HAD BROKEN THE CASTE RULE. WHILE STILL PRESENT WITHIN HINDUISM IN INDIA, THE CASTE SYSTEM IS SLOWLY CHANGING. ONE SPECIFIC EXAMPLE OF CHANGE OCCURRED WHEN MAHATMA GANDHI PROCLAIMED THE UNTOUCHABLES *HARIJANS*, OR CHILDREN OF GOD. DISCRIMINATING AGAINST UNTOUCHABLES IS BANNED UNDER INDIAN LAW.

- A person who practices the religion called Hinduism is called a Hindu.

- Hindus worship in a temple, Hindu center, mandir, or satsangam.

- Hinduism is also known as "Sanatana Dharma," which means "Eternal Teaching."

- A Hindu religious leader is called a priest (brahmin) or a guru.

- Age: About 3,500 years, from the time of the compilation of the Vedas, in 1500 BCE

- Country of origin: India

- Number of American Hindus: 1.5 million

- Number of Hindus worldwide: 900 million

- Time in USA: 170 years

Why I'm Hindu

by Neal A. Chatterjee

There I sat in the midsummer India heat, twelve years old, separated from our family priest by a sacrificial fire fed by *ghee* (Indian butter), surrounded by food offerings to God, my back facing hundreds of family and friends. The heat, the priest's Sanskrit mantras, the low murmur of the people behind me and the distinctive city noises of Calcutta, all seemed to flow through me. At the time, I hadn't truly grasped the significance of this coming-of-age religious rite, or *upanayanam*.

It was a three-day event—two of them devoted to the religious ceremony and the final day to greeting and gathering with the family. The ceremony consisted of many offerings to God, in the form of tangible food items like rice, and verbally through spoken Hindu mantras. It marks the transition of a young Hindu man between the ages of nine and twenty from childhood to a disciplined commitment to the study of religion and education. Many of the agreements that I made during the ceremony included getting up at dawn, not taking any afternoon naps, eating three meals a day, always saving food at the end of meals to offer to animals and poorer individuals, and finally and most importantly, always saying the *gayatri mantra*. This mantra is given from the priest to the young student only during this ceremony, and it is a short three-line verse, which asks

God to bless our pursuit of knowledge and supreme understanding.

The young man also receives a string, which he wears, diagonally, across his upper torso. Each morning and night he must wrap this string around his finger a certain number of times, and then unwrap it each time he says the *gayatri mantra*. The string, metaphorically, serves as a reminder of the commitment that I made to the disciplined study of Hindu religion. Originally, the young Hindu boy would leave his parents' household and travel to the house of a wise sage, or guru. There, he would literally follow the promises he made during this cere-mony. Now these promises are generally interpreted as metaphorical, though the promise to repeat the *gayatri mantra* is still retained. Despite the summer heat and incredible length of the ceremony, I was touched and comforted by all the family and friends who attended the ceremony. On the final day of the three-day event—reserved for celebration—I received countless blessings and helpful instructions for my new path as a Hindu man. It felt as if I was being welcomed into a beautiful, supportive community of individuals, many of whom I barely knew, and it was wonderful.

Being Hindu, and beginning to carefully study the voluminous Hindu scripture, has directed and guided me to become a better person. My studies have directed me to be a better student, to gain a better understanding of my own behavior, to always offer service to my friends and to strangers, to show the utmost respect for teachers and parents, and many other truths. It has also taught me that all reli-gions are truth and have to be respected. I'll end with a passage from the Gita which states that "Just as there are many paths, straight and curved, that lead towards the eventual sea" there are analogously many paths (i.e., religions), straight and curved (i.e., different kinds of people), that lead us to the eventual sea (God).

Why am I losing my faith?

Dear Pastor Paul,

I'm a sophomore in high school who was very strong in Christian beliefs until about a year ago. I met a very wonderful Muslim guy who is now my best friend. Since meeting him, I don't feel connected to God anymore, I don't feel his love, and I certainly don't feel a need for him in my life. I've been questioning everything—from the importance of my religion to the reality of it. Any suggestions?

Dear Friend,

Frankly, I don't see the connection between meeting your wonderful Muslim guy and not feeling connected to God. Many people go through a period of questioning and disconnection from their faith during adolescence. That may be what is going on with you right now. Are you still praying? Are you still going to church? It is important for you to have a supportive Christian community to help you through this difficult period.

Instead of blaming your Muslim friend for losing your faith, use him as a resource. Most Muslims have a very strong faith in God (Allah), and Islam locates its roots in the Patriarch Abraham, as do Jews and Christians. God does love you, and while you may not feel connected to God right now, God feels connected to you. Hopefully, you and your best friend can both grow in each of your faiths as you grow older.

How can I get my boyfriend to stop talking about religion?

Dear Pastor Paul,

My boyfriend and I have very divergent religious views. He was raised Baptist in Latin America, and I was raised in Canada with no religious instruction. When we're not discussing religion, we get along very well, but conversations about faith spring up all the time and often end in an argument about how he sees no future for us because I don't believe what he believes. Is there a way to come to some common ground on this issue? I'd like to ask him not to talk to me about religion at all, but since it's such an important focus in his life I want to share that with him in the ways that I can. Obviously, we aren't the only people to have encountered this problem. How do you make it work?

Dear Friend,

This is going to be tough. You have very different religious outlooks, and while *you* may be happy to live with the difference, *he* is not. You say that these conversations spring up all the time and are unexpected, which means he is thinking about it even more than he is letting you know. It is a real problem for him.

You have two choices: The first requires your boyfriend to soften in his beliefs enough to permit your differences of faith. The second is for you to open yourself to the possibility of a conversion experience to the faith of your boyfriend.

Your boyfriend says he doesn't see a future for you two unless you start to believe what he believes, and you say that you would rather he not talk about religion at all. Interfaith dating (and that is what you are doing) requires a lot of flexibility on both sides, and, unfortunately, I am not sure your relationship is flexible enough.

With more conversation and time, things might work out. But there may come a time when this relationship is not right for either of you.

CHAPTER 5

SCHOOL

Why are there religious high schools?

Dear Pastor Paul,

I met this guy who goes to a Jewish school. Is that very different than my public school? What is the point of a separate religious school if we are all supposed to be the same?

Dear Friend,

Many people are choosing to go to religious schools these days. In most ways, a Jewish school (*yeshiva*) is just like your public school. Young people learn math, history and science, and play sports and do arts, just like in public schools. But in a Jewish school there are additional classes on the Jewish religion, language and culture. Also, the school's behavior guidelines are based on its religious beliefs. Like Catholic schools for Catholics and Muslim schools for Muslims, Jewish schools are important for Jewish families that are concerned with maintaining the religious integrity of their children.

This doesn't make your Jewish friend any different than Jewish, Christian, Muslim or Hindu children who attend your public school. Everyone in America is equal, but we are not all meant to be the same. What makes our country great is the fact that people can learn and practice any religion freely while still being fully American.

Why I'm Zoroastrian

by James R. Williams

Although I was born and raised in a Judeo-Christian world, I am a proud member of an ancient, now small, but vibrant faith. I am Zoroastrian despite being the only member of my faith at each of the schools I have attended. I retain my Zoroastrian customs even though the nearest fire temple is over five-hundred miles away from my home. Yet mostly I am Zoroastrian because of the inner peace, strength and insights that I regularly gain through the practice of being an active member of my faith.

It wasn't until my Navjote—an initiation ceremony somewhat like a Jewish Bar Mitzvah—that I fully became a Zoroastrian. It was then that I truly began to understand and recognize what my religion meant. Prior to my initiation, I knew the three tenets of the religion—Humata, Hukhta, Havarastra (Good Thoughts, Good Words, Good Deeds)—and some of the basic philosophy and prayers. However, it was only after my Navjote at the age of nine that I became a full member of my faith, and thus responsible for all of my own actions. I was thereafter required to perform the daily prayers and wear the *sudreh* and *kusti* (a sacred shirt and thread) that serve as powerful reminders of Zoroastrian teachings. The most significant change of all was personal: For the first time I identified myself as Zoroastrian, and this made me seek out more knowledge of my faith and a greater attachment to religion in general.

Today I turn to Zarathushtra's wise teachings as a way of life with my belief in Ahura Mazda as the one omniscient, omnipotent God as the keystone. As a Zoroastrian, I am called upon to exercise my free will to do good, to choose the path of righteousness over the path of evil. The calling to fill my life with good thoughts, words and deeds is something that I take seriously and is why I have dedicated my life to public service. My religion's demand that I actively seek a strong ethical and moral code, in thought and practice, is something I strive to uphold constantly. The strength of the Zoroastrian code has allowed this religion to survive centuries of persecution and the successive scatterings of its followers, and its rigorous standards make each Zoroastrian a vital and engaged member of our home community.

JUST THE FAQs
ZOROASTRIANISM

- A person who practices Zoroastrianism is called a Zoroastrian.
- The founder of the Zoroastrian faith is Zoroaster.
- Zoroastrians worship in fire temples.
- Religious leaders are called priests.
- The primary sacred writings are the Avesta.
- Age: 3,500
- Country of origin: Persia, now Iran
- Number of American Zoroastrians: 18,000
- Number of Zoroastrians worldwide: 200,000

Who is a Christian slacker?

Dear Pastor Paul,

I don't know how much you know about See You at the Pole, but it's a yearly gathering of Christian students around the flagpole at school to pray. At my school, the common consensus seems to be that all the "good" Christians participate, but if you're Christian and don't go then you're "not so dedicated" and a Christian slacker. This makes me mad since many who participate only go because it's the "in thing" to do and because you get a T-shirt to prove to everyone that you were there. I'm Christian, and I don't feel I have to prove that to anybody. If we lived in a time when Christianity wasn't the cool thing to do, would See You at the Pole be so popular?

Dear Friend,

As if cliques weren't already stiflingly intense during the high school years! It may not provide any immediate comfort, but the truth is that Christians have been pointing at one another, shouting, "Christian slacker!" since the very beginning. This is why we have Orthodox, Catholic and so many Protestant denominations (well, it is a bit more complicated than that, but you get the idea), as well as the strife these groups experience internally.

The Bible offers many different ways to live out faith. The kids at the flagpole are probably following Matthew 5:1: "Neither do men light a candle, and put it under a bushel, but on a candle-stick; and it gives light to all that are in the house." You are interpreting Matthew 6:5: "And when you pray, do not be as the hypocrites: for they love to pray standing in the house of prayer and in the corners of the streets, that they may be seen of men.

Verily I say unto you, They have their reward." Different types of people will respond differently to the questions of religion. Each should attempt to be as respectful as possible to the other.

The only one who you and the other Christians at your school have to prove anything to is God. Remember: T-shirts with messages on them mean very little; it's what's on the inside that counts. Strive to understand how God is calling you to live, and follow that calling.

CELEBRITY SPIRITUALITY

"The most powerful idea that's entered the world in the last few thousand years—the idea of grace—is the reason I would like to be a Christian. Though, as I said to [U2 guitarist] The Edge one day, I sometimes feel more like a fan, rather than actually in the band. I can't live up to it. But the reason I would like to is the idea of grace. It's really powerful."

Bono, the *Beliefnet* interview by Anthony DeCurtis

- Protestant Christianity is a branch of Christianity.

- A person who practices Protestant Christianity is called a Christian, a Believer, an Evangelical or by the name of their denomination, such as Baptist, Presbyterian or Lutheran.

- Protestant Christians worship in a church.

- A Protestant Christian leader is a minister or reverend.

- The primary sacred writing is the Bible.

- Age: 2,000 years; the Protestant movement in Christianity began in the 1500s.

- Country of origin: Israel/Palestine; Europe

- Number of American Protestant Christians: 100 million

- Number of Protestant/ Evangelical Christians worldwide: 700 million

- Time in USA: 500 years

Why I'm Christian
(Protestant/Evangelical)

by Mikaela R. Tyson

When I was just five years old, I asked my mother what a Christian was, because I'd heard the term used at school. She told me that a Christian was a person who believed that Jesus had died and risen again to take away everyone's sin. By confessing that we are sinful, and then asking Jesus to come into our lives, we could become his followers. I decided that I wanted Jesus in my life, so I said a prayer of confession and acceptance right then and there. My faith hasn't focused on any particular tradition, although in Jamaica, Christianity is so mainstream that most people acknowledge the birth of Christ at Christmas, and his death and resurrection at Easter. However, the most important aspect of my faith is my relationship with God. The idea that the creator of the universe, the author of all life, would humble himself and assume human form, come to Earth in poverty, and suffer the most torturous type of death ever known to humankind on a cross, all because he wanted to re-establish a relationship with me, absolutely blew my mind. The prospect of having God as a best friend compelled me to pursue my relationship with Christ.

Accepting Christ's phenomenal sacrifice was just the first step to having a relationship with God. Like any other friend, I had to spend quality time with him if I wanted our relationship to grow. So I aimed to talk to God daily through prayer, and listen to him by reading his Word. Through this relationship I came to realize that while God had saved me by his grace, faith without works is dead. If I really have a relationship with the all-powerful God of all creation, then my life ought to look different from those who don't. Imitating Christ became my constant goal. I was challenged by the stories of Christ's compassion for the poor and the needy, so I helped to teach children in an inner-city community in Kingston, Jamaica (my hometown). I've strived to emulate Christ's humility, selflessness and genuine love for people, regardless of their social status. I was strengthened by the knowledge that God's Spirit gave me the power to resist the urge to be self-absorbed and even self-righteous. Most importantly, a vibrant relationship with God means that I can't help but to tell others about him. Knowing Christ has affected every single aspect of my life, which means that any-one who knows me eventually discovers how important this friendship with God is to me. My life would have been radically different had I not met Christ at such an early age, and putting my faith in him is a decision I don't regret.

Why won't my friends respect my faith?

Dear Pastor Paul,

Many of my friends have left the Catholic Church, and they want me to "give my life to Jesus" and be "born again." I gave my life to Jesus in my confirmation, and like the 100th lamb, I have strayed—but he has come and taken me back to the fold and he lives in my heart now. One friend asked me if I was "saved," and I couldn't answer yes because I didn't understand the question and knew she would not accept me as I am and leave it!

How do I explain this to my friends?

Dear Friend,

There are many different traditions within Christianity, and each one has its own vocabulary to address its beliefs. Evangelical Christians tend to use phrases like "born again" and "saved" to speak of the experience of accepting Jesus that they have had as an adult. However, in other traditions—notably Catholic and Eastern Orthodox—being a Christian begins at birth and continues with a number of steps along the way, including first communion and confirmation as well as adult conversions. Inform your friends about your own encounters with Jesus Christ and the path that you have taken in the Catholic Church. Your friends should recognize the integrity of your fine Catholic tradition and accept you.

Why I'm Roman Catholic
by Nicholas Joshua Teh

I didn't quite grow up Catholic. I was the result of a mixed marriage and some curious negotiations between the parties involved. My father—who is Evangelical Protestant—had gotten it into his head that I should only be baptized when I had reached an age of sufficient reason to choose a church for myself; that I would be all the better for it. My Catholic mother, on the other hand, sent me off to Sunday school with the rest of the cradle Catholics and brought me to Mass on Sundays. I do not think she ever had a doubt that my church would be her church. Still, she complied with my father's wishes, and I was not baptized til I was about fourteen. Along the road to Catholicism, I had the good fortune to be granted some marvelous intuitions about God and his love. I have never been a skeptic, and being in God's presence was an understanding I gravitated toward from my youngest days. However, good intuitions were hardly enough to influence my mindset; by the time I was eleven I had begun to subscribe to a vague, tortured sort of nihilism with all its attendant self-pity.

So it was against this backdrop that I had my first real spiritual experience. It happened at a Redemptorist Mission camp. It was charismatic in form, as it probably had to be for me; my destructive and false perceptions had to be exposed by the light of the Holy Spirit. I experienced what some would call a "healing" experience, and along with it, peace in the knowledge that my destiny lay with this Trinitarian God who was calling me to himself. It was then that I felt a burning desire to be baptized into the Roman Catholic Church. But first I had to be informed, so I read whatever I could get my hands on: St. Augustine, Scott Hahn, St. Thomas More, various Catholic and Protestant apologists, etc. I was quite aware that my initial, emotionally charged spiritual jumpstart needed a solid foundation if I were going to respond to God's call. I began to pray and read the Bible seriously. The more I pursued these activities, the more I became convinced that the Catholic Church painted the most compelling picture of the mystery of human existence. It presented an eminently reasonable worldview—one in which philosophy made provisions for theology and theology did the same for mysticism. Soon enough, I was certain that the Catholic Church was Christ's church and that it taught and led the faithful with the authority that comes from speaking the absolute truth. When my baptism finally took place, it was a tremendous confluence of my intellectual, spiritual and emotional growth as a

JUST THE FAQs
CATHOLICISM

- The Roman Catholic Church is a branch of Christianity.

- Catholics are called Catholic or Roman Catholic.

- The founder of the faith is Jesus Christ.

- Catholics worship in a church.

- Catholic religious leaders are called priest, bishop or father.

- The sacred text is the Bible.

- Age: 2,000 years

- Country of origin: Israel/Palestine; Rome

- Number of Catholics in America: 51 million

- Number of Catholics worldwide: 1 billion

- Time in USA: 500 years

Christian. I still regard my assent to that sacrament (with the aid of grace, no doubt) as the best of my intentional actions.

Ever since, I've tried to be a contemplative in the world. Catholicism provides the truth about God's plan of salvation for man, and I attempt to better myself through continual self-examination in light of that plan. Of course, no one lights a lamp and hides it, so I try to serve others by helping them to their end—eternal friendship with Christ.

Can God make me smarter?

Dear Pastor Paul,

My brother, who is two years older than me, was a total straight-A student and is going to one of the best colleges in the country next year. I always get at least one grade below his, and it makes me feel like a failure. So my question is, why does God make some people smarter and more talented?

Dear Friend,

High school grades are not the final word on success. You may be a late bloomer who will really hit his stride in college, in graduate school or in the workforce. So it's a little early to label yourself a failure. If you start telling yourself that you're not smart at this young age, then you're setting yourself up to live a life that fulfills your own expectations. Remember, it's never too late to exhibit excellence.

God makes people smart in different ways. God doesn't need all of us to be physicists or top-level lawyers. God wants you to be smart and fulfilled in your own way, utilizing your unique combination of skills and passions. Instead of asking why God made your brother smarter than you, begin to search within yourself for what ideas and activities fascinate you, and focus on those. You'll find you're smarter than you thought.

Why are my friends down on me for praying at school?

Dear Pastor Paul,

I used to pray before lunch at school, but people made fun of me. So I stopped praying out loud and now pray silently. I feel guilty about this because I'm hiding my religious beliefs as if I'm ashamed of them. Is this the right thing to do?

Dear Friend,

Ask yourself if you communicate better with God aloud or silently, because both are acceptable ways to pray. People who prefer to pray silently do so because that's how they best communicate with God, not because they're ashamed of their beliefs. If you prayed aloud because that's how you best communicate with God, then start praying aloud again.

If you're still concerned about getting teased by your peers, then find some place private to pray before heading to lunch. And remember, those kids who make fun of you are probably just uncomfortable with things they don't understand—in this case, your praying. If you feel moved to pray aloud (for God's ears alone, no one likes a religious show-off) in front of your classmates, then in rising above their small-mindedness you may unwittingly become a role model.

HUMILITY

IT IS HUMILITY THAT EXALTS ONE AND FAVORS
HIM AGAINST HIS FRIENDS.

African Proverb

✦

SUCCESSFUL INDEED ARE THE BELIEVERS
WHO ARE HUMBLE IN THEIR PRAYERS,
AND WHO SHUN VAIN CONVERSATION,
AND WHO ARE PAYERS OF THE POOR-DUE,
AND WHO GUARD THEIR MODESTY.

Islam

✦

THE LAMENTER WHO IS SEEKING A VISION CRIES,
FOR HE IS HUMBLING HIMSELF,
REMEMBERING HIS NOTHINGNESS IN THE PRESENCE
OF THE GREAT SPIRIT.

Sioux Tradition

✦

WITHIN THE WORLD
THE PALACE PILLAR IS BROAD,
BUT THE HUMAN HEART
SHOULD BE MODEST.

Shinto

Be humble, be harmless,
Have no pretension,
Be upright, forbearing;
Serve your teacher in true obedience,
Keeping the mind and body in cleanness,
Tranquil, steadfast, master of ego,
Standing apart from the things of the senses,
Free from self;
Aware of the weakness in mortal nature.

Hinduism

✦

Blessed are the meek, for they shall inherit the earth.

Christianity

✦

Subdue pride by modesty, overcome hypocrisy by simplicity,
and dissolve greed by contentment.

Jainism

✦

For the natural man is an enemy to God,
and has been from the fall of Adam, and will be, forever
and ever, unless he yields to the enticings of the Holy Spirit,
and puts off the natural man and becomes a saint
through the atonement of Christ the Lord, and becomes
as a child, submissive, meek, humble, patient, full of love,
willing to submit to all things which the Lord sees fit to
inflict upon him, even as a child submits to his father.

Church of Jesus Christ of Latter-Day Saints

CONFUCIUS SAID, "A GENTLEMAN DOES NOT
GRIEVE THAT PEOPLE DO NOT RECOGNIZE HIS MERITS;
HE GRIEVES AT HIS OWN INCAPACITIES."

Confucianism

◆

TO KNOW WHEN ONE DOES NOT KNOW IS BEST.
TO THINK ONE KNOWS WHEN ONE DOES
NOT KNOW IS A DIRE DISEASE.

Taoism

◆

THE FOOL WHO KNOWS THAT HE IS A FOOL
IS FOR THAT VERY REASON A WISE MAN;
THE FOOL WHO THINKS HE IS WISE IS CALLED A FOOL INDEED.

Buddhism

Should I fight or turn the other cheek?

Dear Pastor Paul,

What should I do when my friends turn against me to join the enemy team, and then talk against me? I love and respect God, so I walk away, but that makes me feel like I'm being a pushover. It makes me feel like I might be scared of what might happen if I retaliate.

Dear Friend,

Whether you're thinking of responding with physical violence or just fighting fire with fire and talking them down, neither option will make you feel good or solve the problem. Consider instead the spiritual approach Jesus outlines in the Bible: Love your enemies, do good to those who hate you, bless those who curse you, pray for those who abuse you. If anyone strikes you on the cheek, offer the other also (Luke 6:27–29). Ask yourself what will allow you to live with more love and respect—not only for God (although that is of ultimate importance)—but for yourself as well.

It takes a strong person to choose the nonviolent approach. In walking away you are not being "a pushover"; instead you are following a deep spiritual path set out by Jesus and followed by people such as Gandhi and Martin Luther King Jr., who also used nonviolent alternatives to achieving the goal of love and respect for God and for themselves.

If you show this spiritual strength, you will draw closer to God and also attract friends who are rooted in the same principles of love and respect as you are.

JUSTICE

BELIEVERS, FULFILL YOUR DUTIES TO ALLAH AND BEAR TRUE WITNESS.
DO NOT ALLOW YOUR HATRED FOR OTHER MEN
TO TURN AWAY FROM JUSTICE.
DEAL JUSTLY; JUSTICE IS NEARER TO TRUE PIETY.

The Qur'an

◆

THERE IS ENOUGH FOR EVERYBODY'S NEED,
BUT NOT FOR EVERYBODY'S GREED.

Gandhi

◆

IN GERMANY THEY FIRST CAME FOR THE COMMUNISTS,
AND I DIDN'T SPEAK UP BECAUSE I WASN'T A COMMUNIST.
THEN THEY CAME FOR THE JEWS, AND I DIDN'T SPEAK UP BECAUSE
I WASN'T A JEW. THEN THEY CAME FOR THE TRADE UNIONISTS,
AND I DIDN'T SPEAK UP BECAUSE I WASN'T A TRADE UNIONIST.
THEN THEY CAME FOR THE CATHOLICS, AND I DIDN'T SPEAK UP
BECAUSE I WAS A PROTESTANT. THEN THEY CAME FOR ME,
AND BY THAT TIME NO ONE WAS LEFT TO SPEAK UP.

Pastor Martin Niemoller

◆

IF I AM NOT FOR MYSELF, WHO WILL BE FOR ME?
IF I AM NOT FOR OTHERS, WHO AM I FOR?
AND IF NOT NOW, WHEN?

Rabbi Hillel

PEACE, IN THE SENSE OF ABSENCE OF WAR,
IS OF LITTLE VALUE TO SOMEONE WHO IS DYING OF HUNGER
OR COLD. PEACE CAN ONLY LAST WHERE HUMAN RIGHTS
ARE RESPECTED, WHERE PEOPLE ARE FED, AND WHERE
INDIVIDUALS AND NATIONS ARE FREE.

The Fourteenth Dalai Lama

PEACE IS THE WORK OF JUSTICE INDIRECTLY,
IN SO FAR AS JUSTICE REMOVES THE OBSTACLES TO PEACE;
BUT IT IS THE WORK OF CHARITY (LOVE) DIRECTLY, SINCE CHARITY,
ACCORDING TO ITS VERY NOTION, CAUSES PEACE.

Thomas Aquinas

THERE MAY BE TIMES WHEN WE ARE POWERLESS
TO PREVENT INJUSTICE, BUT THERE MUST NEVER BE A TIME
WHEN WE FAIL TO PROTEST.

Elie Wiesel

CELEBRITY SPIRITUALITY

"You grow by attempting to get out of your comfort zone. To push yourself in areas where you might be afraid. To have a little faith—replace fear with faith. That's something I try to do. I was given a Buddhist amulet by two of the girls working on the film *City of Ghosts*. I still wear it. The positioning of the hands on a Buddha mean something, each one different. This one had its hands positioned to protect me from fear. I like what it stands for: That fear is really the enemy. It reminds me, whenever I'm afraid, to replace it with a faith that things will work out."

Matt Dillon in the *Beliefnet* interview by Paul O'Donnell

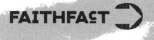
Does God like one sports team more than another?

Dear Pastor Paul,

Some friends of mine are on the basketball team at my high school. They are serious Christians, and a group of them prays before the game. Now, I don't mind people being religious, but that makes me uncomfortable. Do you think it's okay for a team to pray to beat another team? Should people pray just for a game?

Dear Friend,

Petitioning God for God's help is fine in my book, even in a sports match. However, it would be wrong if a team used prayer to God as a trump card to win a match. Prayer should witness to the world that even though these athletes are at the top of their game, they still know that the ultimate power is in God's hands. I'm pretty sure God does not care which team wins, as long as both teams exhibit good sportsmanship and play to the best of their God-given abilities.

Sports

Because we tend to think of the spirit as separate from the body, we rarely link spirituality with sports and athletics. But sports can fulfill some of the basic definitions of spirituality: For example, they connect individuals to something larger than themselves. On the field, the goals of the individual become completely integrated with the team's goals. Or, take the amazing mystical experience called "the zone," or flow. The zone is a term athletes use to talk about the complete union they sometimes feel while playing their sport, when the athlete is totally open to the present moment. That sense of the zone would be familiar to someone who was knowledgeable in the Way, or the *Tao*. The Tao is the energy that flows through all things. When the athlete taps into that force, she or he becomes capable of feats that could never be accomplished through individual intelligence or strength.

Another spiritual concept integral to sports is endurance. Endurance is that voice that says *yes* when everything else is telling you to give up. One of the sports world's most inspiring figures is champion bicyclist Lance Armstrong. A world-class athlete, ranked number one in the world, Armstrong was poised to win the ultimate prize, the Tour de France, when he was diagnosed with cancer and given a 50/50 chance to live. He went through a traumatic time of medical operations and recovery. He refused to listen to the voices that said *no*. Since then he has won the Tour de France a record six times, drawing on the endurance he built during his convalescence. The discipline that comes with participating in athletics can inform your spiritual practice, if you stay positive until the finish line.

Spiritual Activity #1
What team are you on?

Identify all the teams you are a part of: sports teams, a study group, at work, etc. Think about your place on that team and how you tune into the goals of the whole group. Consciously remove your ego from the equation and see how that affects your performance and the performance of others. Imagine expanding your definition of a team to include all living beings and extend to them the compassion, or feeling for others, for those who are your "real" team members.

Spiritual Activity #2
Get into the zone.

Identify the experience of "the zone" or "flow" in your life. Any sport or athletic activity is an opportunity to experience the zone. After a game or practice, consider those moments when you rose to a challenge, or when your ability flowed without being forced. Watch for it in sports on TV. Notice when a player seems unable to miss the hoop, or makes a no-look pass. Remind yourself of the constant possibility that tapping into "the flow" is all around us. You may wish to read more about the Tao in the sacred book called the *Tao Te Ching*. Or learn more about the flow in books called *Flow* and *Flow in Sports* by Mihaly Csikszentmihalyi.

Spiritual Activity #3
Just do it!

Work on your physical endurance to nurture your spiritual endurance. Start by walking or jogging a quarter of a mile every day for a week. Add a quarter mile each week until you build up to three miles. See if you can build up your stamina as well as the voice inside you that says, "Yes. I can do this." If you are an advanced athlete, push through the times when you feel like quitting. (Make sure, of course, that you know your body's limits.) Your body's endurance can translate into a positive attitude. Saying yes to life is sometimes the most profound spiritual choice we can make, and it sets an example for those around us who are going through hard times. You can help someone who needs some positive endurance by being the voice that says, "Yes, you can do this" to help them along.

CHAPTER 6

SEX, DRUGS & ROCK 'N' ROLL

Can I keep my virginity and my boyfriend?

Dear Pastor Paul,

I'm sixteen years old and have decided to stay a virgin until I get married. I recently met a great new guy who I care about a lot. He doesn't go to my school, and he doesn't know my feelings and my commitments. I'm so afraid to tell him because I might lose him over this. I know if he really loves me, he'll respect me, but that's easier said than done. How can I ask him to have a sexless relationship when so many other girls will be more than happy to oblige?

Dear Friend,

Where have you been hiding? Don't you know that virginity is in? Everyone is speaking out about and pledging to maintain their virginity until marriage. It is totally cool and okay to not have sex if that is what you are comfortable with, and that makes the boyfriend question easy. No person is worth compromising your own integrity for. Without being self-righteous (nobody likes that), set your personal moral standard and make sure your friends and boyfriends live up to it—or find new ones who will.

As far as breaking it to the boyfriend, think of all the great things you are going to offer him in the relationship: your friendship, your beautiful presence, someone on his side, your love, your affection—all of these things he gains by staying with you. If your boyfriend is just after sex, then he'll likely take off—that's just proof he wasn't the right guy for you. Fear not, and be patient—there are plenty of guys who are looking for exactly who you are.

What The Religions Say About PREMARITAL SEX

Buddhism

The third of the five precepts suggest that people should be responsible sexually. Sex is not in itself "bad"; however, it is part of what makes up *samsara*, or the world of illusion. Desire and attachments to sex, whether it is within or outside of marriage, are obstacles to achieving complete enlightenment.

Christianity

Conservative Christians prohibit sex outside of marriage, while more liberal traditions have a tolerant view if the sex is between consenting adults and the partners use protection against diseases such as AIDS.

Hinduism

 In Hinduism, sexual pleasure is considered part of *kama*, one of the Hindu's four life goals. That is where the name of the *Kama Sutra*, an ancient Indian text about sex, comes from. However, Hindu *dharma*, or duty, suggests that sexual activity should be limited to the *grhastha ashrama*, or married stage of life.

Islam

 Sex is forbidden in Islam outside of marriage.

Judaism

Judaism traditionally prohibits sex outside of marriage, though many modern Jews, especially in the more liberal denominations, have a more tolerant view if both are adults and the partners use protection against diseases such as AIDS.

Is it okay to have a lesbian crush on my best friend?

Dear Pastor Paul,

I am a Catholic schoolgirl. For a while now I have been having feelings for my friend, and she has the same feelings. I've told my dad how I feel, and he says it's just a phase, but I think it's more than that. She says she has great opportunities with a guy, but a recent e-mail I got from her says she still wants "something to do w/me" relationship-wise. I'm so confused. Please give me some good advice!

Dear Friend,

Well, it sounds like you are pretty comfortable with your feelings for your friend so I won't take time to say that your feelings are okay—they are—because you already know that. Your dad is right in a way. Some people have affectionate/sexual desires for people of the same gender that don't last after adolescence, while others know they will love people of the same gender for their whole lives. Your friend might be one of those people who wants to experiment with you but is really more interested in the opposite sex. I see a red flag when she says she has a "great opportunity with a guy," as if that would be more important than an opportunity with you. Hold out for a friend who will love you fully.

(NOTE: *Many religious leaders do not agree with me on the question of whether or not it is a sin to be gay or lesbian. I believe that God loves all of God's children equally—including those created gay and lesbian. Readers should know that there are others who feel differently. You will have to decide for yourself.*)

What The Religions Say About HOMOSEXUALITY

Buddhism

 Homosexuality is not a big issue in Buddhism. Although there are some texts and leaders that speak of it as a negative action, the Buddha never mentioned it and neither did the philosophers who immediately followed him. Sexual activity, whether heterosexual or homosexual, is not morally judged. Lesbian and gay Buddhists find comfort in the high value placed on questioning teachings that are not relevant to one's own life. The Buddha said, "Do not go by what is handed down, nor by the authority of your traditional teachings. When you know of yourselves, 'These teachings are good, or not good,' only then accept or reject them." Though the Dalai Lama has sometimes spoken out against homosexual relationships, in recent years he and other leaders in the West have shown a willingness to talk to leading gay and lesbian Buddhists about reexamining traditional teachings on homosexuality, and there is a general acceptance of lesbians and gays in American Buddhist life.

Christianity

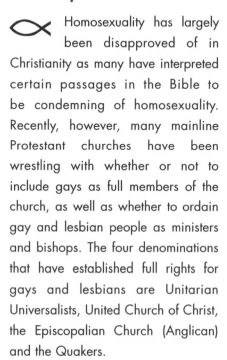 Homosexuality has largely been disapproved of in Christianity as many have interpreted certain passages in the Bible to be condemning of homosexuality. Recently, however, many mainline Protestant churches have been wrestling with whether or not to include gays as full members of the church, as well as whether to ordain gay and lesbian people as ministers and bishops. The four denominations that have established full rights for gays and lesbians are Unitarian Universalists, United Church of Christ, the Episcopalian Church (Anglican) and the Quakers.

The Christian debate over homosexuality often hinges on how people view scripture and the passages in question—with more conservative Christians and fundamentalists viewing the Bible as literally true for all times and all people, and more moderates viewing the Bible as open to interpretation based on the time it was written, the progress of science and the experience of the individual person. The Metropolitan Community Church is a Christian denomination founded by gay people that has churches throughout the country and worldwide. Within most Christian denominations there are groups that offer support to lesbian and gay congregants.

Hinduism

Hinduism doesn't support or condemn homosexuality. There are conservative Hindus who ignore or disapprove of homosexuality, or argue that Hinduism teaches that giving in to sensual pleasures of any kind will impede one's continuation on the spiritual path. However, Hinduism's general tolerance of different approaches to God often extends to an understanding of gays and lesbians. Some Hindu gay groups argue for the Vedic concept of third sex or gender known as *tritiya-prakriti*. For example, one form of the God Shiva, known as Ardhanarishwara, is half male and half female.

Islam

Gays and lesbians are generally not accepted in Islamic society. The Qur'an does not expressly forbid homosexuality, but traditional Islam does prohibit indecency and lewd behavior. However, as in Christianity and Judaism, there are groups being formed to support gay Muslims. The Al-Fatiha Foundation, based in Washington D.C., for example, provides support to gay and lesbian Muslims.

Judaism

There is a wide range of opinions concerning gays and lesbians in the Jewish community. Although there are passages within the Torah that have been interpreted to condemn homosexuality, many Jews allow for reinterpretation of these laws in contemporary times. Within the Reform denomination, and increasingly in the Conservative denomination, there is acceptance for gays and lesbians. The Reform and Reconstructionist denominations ordain openly gay rabbis.

Can I be tattooed and still be Jewish?

Dear Pastor Paul,

Okay, here's the deal—I'm Jewish, and while I am not hugely observant, I am proud of my heritage. Only one thing—my parents tell me that Jews don't get tattoos, and I really want one. In fact, I want many. Will I not be Jewish if I get a tattoo?

Dear Friend,

Your parents are right: Traditional Judaism prohibits tattoos, and you may be restricted from being buried in some Jewish cemeteries because of it. This is not to say that you will "not be Jewish" if you get a tattoo. Reform Jews have a more open approach to tattoos than Orthodox Jews because they do not see the Torah passages against it as an essential law. However, I suggest you respect your parents' wishes until you move out of their house. It may interest you to know that Muslims also prohibit tattoos.

TATTOOING & PIERCING

Buddhism

While there is no prohibition against tattooing or piercing in Buddhism, Buddhists believe one should be respectful of the body and the consequence of every action. Each person should determine the relevance of the teachings on tattooing and piercing to their own life.

Christianity

Christianity does not have one strict approach to tattooing and piercing. Some Evangelical Christians call for modesty in appearance and disapprove of tattooing, while others view tattooing as a way of advertising their faith and have tattoos of Jesus as well as quotes from the Bible.

Hinduism

Tattooing and piercing are not prohibited in Hinduism, and some Hindus view them favorably as a symbolic devotional device or way of testing the body. Decorating the body with *henna*, a form of temporary tattooing, is an important Hindu marriage tradition.

Islam

Traditional Muslims do not approve of body modification of any kind, or symbolic representation on the skin.

Judaism

Traditional Judaism forbids tattooing based upon personal modesty before God as well as the passage, "You shall not make gashes in your flesh for the dead, or incise any marks on yourselves: I am the Lord" (Leviticus 19:28). Many Jews will not allow a tattooed body to be buried in a Jewish cemetery. Today, many young people who identify themselves as Jewish do have tattoos and piercings.

Is masturbation a sin?

Dear Pastor Paul,

   Is masturbation a sin? I've read so many contradictory things, and I'm confused. I can't find anything that tells me where the church actually stands on it. Any light you could shed would be awesome.

Dear Friend,

   Traditionally, Christianity has not been very sympathetic to sexual activity, apart from reproductive sex inside marriage, and that negativity pretty much extends to masturbation. However, there is no explicit mention of it in the Bible as bad or good. That said, many Christians have interpreted certain scripture passages as a divine prohibition against masturbation and have backed up their belief with church teaching. At the same time, some mainline Christian groups consider masturbation to be a harmless activity and not inherently sinful.

   While Christians will never agree on whether masturbation is a sin, most will agree that a sin is any act that alienates us from God. Does masturbation do this? Well, Jesus commands us to love God and love one another. Masturbation can be a little, uh, self-involved. I put masturbation in the same category as drinking alcohol. It's an activity many people engage in, whether they publicly acknowledge it or not. Done occasionally, it's fine. But don't make a habit of it; at that point it distracts you from God. You have to decide whether or not masturbation is a sin for you in your life.

What The Religions Say About MASTURBATION

Buddhism

Masturbation is not in and of itself wrong. However, the path to Buddhist enlightenment includes five precepts—the third of those is to be responsible sexually. Masturbation may be a distraction from enlightenment. Buddha prohibited nuns and monks from masturbating because they are supposed to lead a celibate and chaste life.

Christianity

Conservative Christians disapprove of masturbation, while more liberal Christians view it as a natural act.

Hinduism

Hindu scriptures do not forbid masturbation, but it is believed this activity may diminish a person's ability to follow the yogic path.

Islam

Traditional Islamic thought considers masturbation *haram*, or forbidden. It is thought of as an impure act and is discouraged.

Judaism

There is a passage in the Torah which has been used to condemn masturbation, and Orthodox Judaism does prohibit it. However Reform and Conservative rabbis do not forbid it in moderation.

How can I get clean and sober?

Dear Pastor Paul,

Because I'm Jewish, I feel like a freak asking you my question but I have respect for all clergy and devout people. I am eighteen years old, a smoker and drug addict with an eating disorder. I've been this way for about six years. I love my religion, find comfort in spirituality and actually aspire to the rabbinate.

The things I believe are good and true. They are not reflected in the way I treat myself, and I hate myself for it—which makes me treat myself worse. I need to stop, but don't know how. I've been through treatment, and I don't want to give up, but I don't feel like I know how to be good and healthy and true.

I thought that people of all religions must struggle with issues about how they act and how they wish they could be. My family has given up, and I understand why. I'm very alone, I'm desperate and want to know what to do.

Dear Friend,

You are going to make a great rabbi once you come through this hard time. Did you ever think that what you are going through is just the experience that God wanted you to have in preparation for your rabbinical training? You now know what it is to suffer in the face of addiction and loneliness. That will make you a more compassionate, patient and wise religious leader for the people in your congregation when you come out on the other side.

But before any of that happens you must deal with your addictions. It will not be easy. It will take courage, commitment and really hard work. But you are not the first one to go through this, and you are not alone. You have to let people help you to help yourself—which may be another lesson God has for you to learn. Check out a local AA chapter in your hometown, or go online to *www.jacsweb.org* for Jews in Recovery.

THE 12 STEPS OF ALCOHOLICS ANONYMOUS

STEPS COMMONLY USED BY PEOPLE ADDICTED TO ALCOHOL ARE:

1. We admitted we were powerless over alcohol—that our lives had become unmanageable.

2. Came to believe that a power greater than ourselves could restore us to sanity.

3. Made a decision to turn our will and our lives over to the care of God as we understood him.

4. Made a searching and fearless moral inventory of ourselves.

5. Admitted to God, to ourselves and to another human being the exact nature of our wrongs.

6. Were entirely ready to have God remove all these defects of character.

7. Humbly asked him to remove our shortcomings.

8. Made a list of all persons we had harmed and became willing to make amends to them all.

9. Made direct amends to such people wherever possible, except when to do so would injure them or others.

10. Continued to take personal inventory, and when we were wrong, promptly admitted it.

11. Sought through prayer and meditation to improve our conscious contact with God as we understood him, praying only for knowledge of His will for us and the power to carry that out.

12. Having had a spiritual awakening as the result of these Steps, we tried to carry this message to alcoholics and to practice these principles in all our affairs.

Will drugs bring me closer to God?

Dear Pastor Paul,

I need to ask what you think about drugs and God. Is getting high a way to experience God or have a spiritual experience?

Dear Friend,

There are a few religions in the world that include mind-altering substances as part of their rituals—perhaps the most famous being the Rastafarian religion, which includes smoking pot, or ganja, as part of a wider religious worldview. However, most religions teach that drugs provide a temporary illusion, not a true perception of reality or the divine. Even if drugs were not illegal and addictive, I would suggest that you practice more meditation and prayer without drugs if you want a true experience of God.

What The Religions Say About ALCOHOL & DRUGS

Buddhism

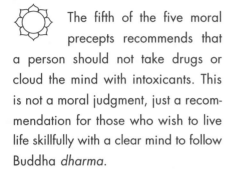 The fifth of the five moral precepts recommends that a person should not take drugs or cloud the mind with intoxicants. This is not a moral judgment, just a recommendation for those who wish to live life skillfully with a clear mind to follow Buddha *dharma*.

Christianity

Many conservative Protestant Christian groups prohibit drinking alcohol, while Catholic, Orthodox and liberal Protestants allow alcohol consumption in moderation and some include consumption of small amounts of wine in liturgies. Drugs are prohibited in Christianity.

Hinduism

Alcohol is tolerated in moderation in Hinduism, though many Hindus refrain from drinking as well. Those who are seriously engaged in spiritual pursuits should avoid it, while others may partake in moderation.

Islam

 Any intoxicating substance is considered a sin in Islam.

Judaism

The consumption of wine is part of the ritual life in Judaism—there is even a separate blessing for wine that is said every *Shabbat* (the Jewish Sabbath). However, moderation is encouraged. Drugs are prohibited.

Does God mind hard rock?

Dear Pastor Paul,

I am a totally devout Christian, and love the Lord with all my heart and soul. He is number one in my life. But I like to listen to Limp Bizkit and other music with cursing—AC/DC, Metallica and others. Is it okay for me to listen to that kind of music as long as I don't repeat the curse words and it doesn't pull me away from God?

Dear Friend,

I'm not going to condemn you for listening to hard rock. I listen to rock music. It sounds like you're aware of the potential of moving away from God and are maintaining your admirable devotion to the Lord. Just pay special attention that the swear words—and stereotypes—don't enter into your everyday vocabulary (it makes you sound dumb and can maybe even start to affect your thinking).

Take the time to explore what about this music interests you and see the connections between that and your faith. I know that frustration, anger, betrayal and confusion are parts of life that hard rock explores—and that Christian leaders often avoid. Just so you know, God understands these emotions too, and is with you during hard times as well as good ones.

Music

Long before people wrote down sacred stories on tablets or books, they passed sacred wisdom along in songs, from group to group and from one generation to the next. Spiritual music is easy to access these days: Just turn on your radio. Artists like Bono (of U2), rappers DMX and Mos Def, Bob Marley, Moby, and Ben Harper all make music that is explicitly spiritual, even though they may not consider their music religious. If you listen carefully, you may find the prophets that speak most directly to your heart may already be on your CD player.

Spiritual Activity #1
Groove to the Spirit.

Listen for spirituality in the music on the radio and in your CD collection. Write out the lyrics to your favorite songs that hold special meaning for you. Burn a CD with songs that are spiritually important to you. Try creating a CD every six months or so to see how your music and beliefs evolve. Have some friends over and play your CDs of spiritual music for each other and talk about why they are so important to you.

Spiritual Activity #2
The sound of the Spirit.

Make music yourself. Not everyone is meant to play the piano or guitar perfectly, but everyone can sing in a choir or learn basic drum beats in a drum circle. As in art, each of us has our own contribution to make to the world through music, and the very process of creating is a spiritual act.

Can Britney still be a Christian?

Dear Pastor Paul,

A few years ago I heard that Britney Spears was a Christian. I was proud of that, because I am a Christian too and was really into her music. But now I am upset about the way she has been dressing and acting, not to mention that her songs talk more and more about sex. How can she be a Christian and act the way she does?

Dear Friend,

I've had these same thoughts, not about Britney Spears, but about hip-hop artists I admired who talked about their Christian faith but didn't seem to "act right." I think the pressures on famous artists to have a certain kind of public persona is very strong. Trying to balance what their faith tells them and what life in the music industry demands is very difficult. While it's not up to us to make excuses for Britney or anyone else, remember that no one is perfect. We are all a work in progress, and we should not judge others lest we be judged ourselves. If you find the mainstream music business not to your taste, you might check out artists in the Christian music industry. They and their music may be more consistent with your personal sense of ethics.

CELEBRITY SPIRITUALITY

"So for three or four years I tried to be what I thought was a good contemporary, conventional Christian. At the time I really felt Christians were right, and everybody else was wrong. But then as time went on, I started to see the world for what it is, which is a very complicated place. And I realized, as much as I love Christ and the teachings of Christ, I can't call myself a Christian, because to call yourself a Christian implies a certainty that I don't have. I think that the world is too old and too complicated for me to say what is right about it and what is wrong."

Moby in the *Beliefnet* interview by Paul Raushenbush

READER/CUSTOMER CARE SURVEY

We care about your opinions! Please take a moment to fill out our online Reader Survey at **http://survey.hcibooks.com**.
As a **"THANK YOU"** you will receive a **VALUABLE INSTANT COUPON** towards future book purchases as well as a **SPECIAL GIFT** available only online! Or, you may mail this card back to us and we will send you a copy of our exciting catalog with your valuable coupon inside.

(PLEASE PRINT IN ALL CAPS)

First Name		MI.		Last Name	

Address				City	

State		Zip		Email:	

1. Gender
- ❑ Female
- ❑ Male

2. Age
- ❑ 8 or younger
- ❑ 9-12
- ❑ 13-16
- ❑ 17-20
- ❑ 21-30
- ❑ 31+

3. Did you receive this book as a gift?
- ❑ Yes
- ❑ No

4. How did you find out about the book
- ❑ Store Display
- ❑ Online
- ❑ Book Club/Mail Order
- ❑ Price Club (Sam's Club, Costco's, etc.)
- ❑ Retail Store (Target, Wal-Mart, etc.)
- ❑ Friend
- ❑ School
- ❑ Parent

- ❑ Online
- ❑ Store Display
- ❑ Teen Magazine
- ❑ Interview/Review

5. Where do you usually buy books
(please choose one)
- ❑ Bookstore
- ❑ Online
- ❑ Book Club/Mail Order
- ❑ Price Club (Sam's Club, Costco's, etc.)
- ❑ Retail Store (Target, Wal-Mart, etc.)

6. What magazines do you like to read *(please choose one)*
- ❑ Teen People
- ❑ Seventeen
- ❑ YM
- ❑ Cosmo Girl
- ❑ Rolling Stone
- ❑ Teen Ink
- ❑ Christian Magazines

7. What books do you like to read *(please choose one)*
- ❑ Fiction
- ❑ Self-help
- ❑ Reality Stories/Memoirs
- ❑ Sports
- ❑ Series Books (Chicken Soup, Fearless, etc.)

8. What attracts you most to a book
(please choose one)
- ❑ Title
- ❑ Cover Design
- ❑ Author
- ❑ Content

TAPE IN MIDDLE; DO NOT STAPLE

BUSINESS REPLY MAIL

FIRST-CLASS MAIL PERMIT NO 45 DEERFIELD BEACH, FL

POSTAGE WILL BE PAID BY ADDRESSEE

HCI Teens
3201 SW 15th Street
Deerfield Beach FL 33442-9875

FOLD HERE

Comments

CHAPTER 7

FORGIVENESS & PRAYER

 FAITHFAST 77% of college students in the USA pray.

Can I pray for what I want?

Dear Pastor Paul,

I have a funny question: Can I pray for what I want? I know this sounds strange, but while I know that we can ask God for what we want, I also don't want to seem selfish or greedy. What do you think?

Dear Friend,

In an interview with the musician Moby, I asked him about prayer. He said that he prayed for what he wanted, even to have a record of his released on a certain label. But he added, "But it is always qualified by the idea of 'God's will be done and not mine.'"

You might want to view it that way as well. Praying about something or someone means that you care about it enough to lift it to God. So while I would encourage you to pray for what you want, end each prayer with "Thy will be done," meaning God's will. Ultimately, the act of prayer acknowledges our dependence on God. Keep that in mind, and it is likely to make your prayers less selfish.

Prayer

Prayer is the essential spiritual activity for anyone who believes in a power greater than themselves (which I call God).

The act of prayer acknowledges your reliance on God, so prayer is also an act of surrendering your faith in your own power and authority and acknowledging our connection to and dependence upon God. Maintaining your communication and connection to God through prayer is a powerful way to fuel your personal spiritual search.

At its deepest spiritual level, prayer is about communication. Of course, communication can go both ways. While many prayers are about articulating our deepest desires and needs to God, they can also include the act of listening to God for answers. Sometimes we talk and talk, but if we don't shut up and stay still and silent, we cannot make room for hearing the important messages God might be trying to communicate to us.

Prayer can also be a way for you to act with compassion toward your fellow human beings and the Earth. Medical journals have shown that hospital patients who were prayed for have fared better than those who had no one praying for them.

Spiritual Activity #1
Starting to pray . . .

If you do not have a personal prayer practice, it is easy to start. Some people like to kneel when they pray, others prefer to stand and others pray while sitting. Find a place and position where you can comfortably quiet your mind and locate the center of your spiritual being, which many people call their soul. Prayers can be about anything. You may give thanks for all of the blessings you have in your life, such as friends, family, your health and even the food you enjoyed that day. You may also wish to lift up some concerns or troubles that you are experiencing or hopes and desires that you may have. The length of prayer is not as important as maintaining your focus and connection to the Divine. You may wish to end your prayer with "Thy will be done," or some other words that acknowledge your dependence on, and devotion to, the Divine.

Spiritual Activity #2
Learning from your neighbor . . .

Investigate the ways that various religions pray. For example, Muslims pray five times a day, which I find very admirable. You may learn a lot by exploring the praying practices of other faiths.

FAITHFACT 72% of college students in the USA believe that people can reach a higher spiritual plane through meditation and prayer.

What's the difference between prayer and meditation?

Dear Pastor Paul,

I have a friend who is really into meditation. She says it brings her closer to God than any of the prayers she said when she was young, or the ones you usually repeat in church. Can you tell me what the difference between meditation and prayer is?

Dear Friend,

There are many different forms of meditation and prayer, and in some ways they overlap and in others they are different.

In general, prayer can be defined as intentional devotion and communication with God or your higher power. Prayer often involves petitioning God for help, or thanking God for good things. Prayer uses words to convey our feelings and thoughts to God. The language of prayer is sometimes specifically provided by tradition, as in the Lord's Prayer in Christianity, the Sh'ma in Judaism or the Al-Fatiha in Islam. Prayer can also be more spontaneous and conversational, but it is always directed toward God.

If prayer is best described as communication, meditation can be described as concentration and awareness. Common forms of meditation concentrate us on our breath and focus our attention to what is happening around us and within our own mind. Meditation leads to awareness and insight, both about ourselves and also about the world. Depending on the tradition, God may or may not be part of a person's meditation practice.

This is not to say there are not great areas of overlap between meditation and prayer. Some spiritual activities, such as repeating the Hail Mary prayer in the Catholic tradition, repeating a yogic mantra and reciting the Qur'an could be called both prayer and meditation. Meditation can be a great way to focus on God, or for the more mystical people, of communing with God. Prayer is also a great way to concentrate our minds and become more aware of ourselves and the world around us as they relate to God.

My advice to your friend is to use both prayer and meditation to bring herself closer to God.

How can I forgive a former friend who treats me horribly?

Dear Pastor Paul,

I've been best friends with a girl for almost two years now, but now that we're in high school, she's pretty much stopped being the Christian she used to be, and she is doing a lot of things she never did before, like reading suicidal poetry, stuff with guys, having people yell at me and just being downright un-Christian. Because of this, she and I aren't speaking now. The hardest part is that she is leaving next week, and I know I need to forgive her, but with everything that's going on, it's really hard.

Dear Friend,

I'm sorry you have lost your friend, as well as suffered abuse because of her. Your friend sounds like she is going through her own personal hell, and unfortunately she has included you in it. However, she did not ask for your forgiveness, so you don't need to forgive her face-to-face. You're also right that it is not okay to harbor resentment in your heart. My suggestion is that you write her a letter, telling her your memories of being together as friends when you were younger, and telling her you value those times you shared. Tell her you are praying for her to find peace and joy in her life—and then offer those prayers to God. Praying for someone is often the best way to help forgive someone.

FORGIVENESS

SUBVERT ANGER BY FORGIVENESS.

Jainism

✦

WHERE THERE IS FORGIVENESS, THERE IS GOD HIMSELF.

Sikhism

✦

IF YOU EFFACE AND OVERLOOK AND FORGIVE, THEN LO! GOD IS FORGIVING, MERCIFUL.

Islam

✦

THE SUPERIOR MAN TENDS TO FORGIVE WRONGS AND DEALS LENIENTLY WITH CRIMES.

Confucianism

IF YOU ARE OFFERING YOUR GIFT AT THE ALTAR,
AND THERE REMEMBER THAT YOUR BROTHER HAS SOMETHING
AGAINST YOU, LEAVE YOUR GIFT THERE BEFORE THE ALTAR AND GO;
FIRST BE RECONCILED TO YOUR BROTHER, AND
THEN COME AND OFFER YOUR GIFT.

Christianity

✦

YOU SHALL NOT TAKE VENGEANCE OR BEAR
ANY GRUDGE AGAINST THE SONS OF YOUR OWN PEOPLE,
BUT YOU SHALL LOVE YOUR NEIGHBOR AS YOURSELF:
I AM THE LORD.

Judaism and Christianity

✦

IN RECONCILING A GREAT INJURY,
SOME INJURY IS SURE TO REMAIN.
HOW CAN THIS BE GOOD?
THEREFORE THE SAGE HOLDS THE LEFT-HAND TALLY OF A CONTRACT;
HE DOES NOT BLAME OTHERS.
THE PERSON OF VIRTUE ATTENDS TO THE OBLIGATION;
THE PERSON WITHOUT VIRTUE ATTENDS TO THE EXACTIONS.

Taoism

How can I get over
my guilt?

Dear Pastor Paul,

My husband and I were both brought up in church. We were going to wait until we got married to have sex. Then one night we gave in. It was special, but I just did not feel right. I knew it was a sin. Now we're nineteen and married with a one-year-old baby. I know she is a blessing, but it is still hard for me to forgive myself and get back to God. I have been battling this for so long now. It is even affecting my love for my husband. I still feel bad when we are together. I don't know how to tell him. I know God is forgiving, but it is just not that easy for me. What should I do?

Dear Friend,

While you may have made a mistake that night, you have got to get over it. It is becoming poison for you, your husband and your child. Your problem is one of faith. Your obsession with your past shows your distrust of Jesus' promise of forgiveness and also a disregard for the blessings that God has granted you in the form of a husband and a child. There are plenty of women out there who are single mothers, as well as women who would like to have children but who are not able to. You should start every day by thanking God for the forgiveness of your sins and then counting your blessings one by one. And get on with fulfilling the purpose that God has for your life.

GRATITUDE

O, YOU WHO BELIEVE! EAT OF THE GOOD THINGS THAT
WE HAVE PROVIDED FOR YOU, AND BE GRATEFUL TO GOD,
IF IT IS HIM THAT YOU WORSHIP.

The Qur'an

✦

I THANK YOU GOD FOR THIS AMAZING DAY;
FOR THE LEAPING GREENLY SPIRITS OF TREES AND A BLUE
TRUE DREAM OF SKY; AND FOR EVERYTHING THAT IS
NATURAL WHICH IS INFINITE WHICH IS YES.

e. e. cummings

✦

IF THE ONLY PRAYER YOU SAID IN YOUR WHOLE LIFE WAS
"THANK YOU," THAT WOULD SUFFICE.

Meister Eckhart

✦

IF YOU CONCENTRATE ON FINDING WHATEVER
IS GOOD IN EVERY SITUATION, YOU WILL DISCOVER THAT YOUR
LIFE WILL SUDDENLY BE FILLED WITH GRATITUDE,
A FEELING THAT NURTURES THE SOUL.

Rabbi Harold Kushner

✦

GRATITUDE IS NOT ONLY THE GREATEST OF VIRTUES,
BUT THE PARENT OF ALL THE OTHERS.

Cicero

A THANKFUL PERSON IS THANKFUL UNDER
ALL CIRCUMSTANCES. A COMPLAINING SOUL COMPLAINS
EVEN IF HE LIVES IN PARADISE.

Baha'u'llah

◆

O LORD MY GOD,
I WILL GIVE THANKS TO YOU FOREVER.

Psalm 30:12

◆

. . . TO WAKE AT DAWN WITH A WINGED HEART AND
GIVE THANKS FOR ANOTHER DAY OF LOVING.

Kahlil Gibran

How can I make peace
with the dead?

Dear Pastor Paul,

I came home from my grandmother's funeral services recently only to see my uncle rushed to the hospital later that day. Two days later he died. They both died from cancer. After both their deaths, I realized I had never told either one how happy I was to have them in my lives, how grateful I was for them and how much I loved them. I feel very guilty for this. How can I make peace with them and myself?

Dear Friend,

I am very sorry to hear of your loss of two dear family members within such a short period of time. Most of us are unprepared for the death of our loved ones, and when they go, we regret not doing or saying more. Your concern shows me you're a kind, loving person. I know you were a blessing to your grandmother and your uncle in their lives.

I want to suggest that you write both your grandmother and your uncle letters. In the letters, recall your favorite memories of them. Express your thanks for how important they were in your life. Tell them how much you love them. If they are buried nearby, or if you can visit their ashes, you can leave the letters at their gravesites. Offer a prayer thanking God for their lives and reach out to their eternal spirit that still exists in the universe. Finally, take time now to tell other loved ones like your mom and dad how important they are and how thankful you are for them. Enjoy your life and all your blessings now.

CHAPTER 8

TOUGH TIMES

How can I have the strength to go on?

Dear Pastor Paul,

I am a seventeen-year-old junior in high school, and I live with my mom, my stepdad and my three-month-old little girl. My baby's dad and I were never married, and we're not together anymore, but he is in her life. A few months ago I met this really sweet guy. We became friends, and now we're engaged to be married. Well, my mom and I are not doing so well. We fight all the time. She always downgrades me, and I can't handle it anymore. I don't feel good about myself or anything I do right now. I just wish I could give up. Please help me.

Dear Friend,

First of all, don't give up. You have taken on a lot at a very young age, and it is no wonder you feel overwhelmed. Things can get much better if you spend more time on yourself. Because you have responsibilities for your child, high school and your new boyfriend, you may think that you can't take time to care for yourself. Don't believe that. Caring for yourself will help you in all your current relationships.

Take at least ten minutes a day to meditate or pray. Meditation and prayer can lift you out of your day-to-day struggles and give you a new perspective on life. When you meditate, you have a time that is just for you—whether you wish to use that to pray to God or simply sit in silence and focus on your breath is up to you. Either way, the benefits will definitely be worth the ten minutes. You'll feel refreshed, more at peace with yourself and with your mom, and more focused about the important decisions you are making.

I also urge you to find a spiritual or religious community that will be loving and supportive to you and your family.

CELEBRITY SPIRITUALITY

"My parents raised us with two specific guiding principles. One, to be open and understanding of the diversity of life. We were taught at a very young age to meditate. When I first learned to meditate at five years old, my father would reward me with a dollar if I stayed quiet for the full five minutes. That eventually evolved to a more traditional technique. And over twenty years later, I am addicted. Meditation really is that first lesson in action—supplying yourself with some silence—so that you can see the complexity of life with some clarity. Two, my dad always told us, 'Never take life too seriously. We're here to learn and to live. So have some fun!' I think that one is pretty easy to understand."

Gotham Chopra in the *Beliefnet* interview by Paul Raushenbush

Meditation

Many of us are so busy that we're sure we don't have time for "extra stuff" like meditating. The truth is that meditation not only helps you to be more spiritual, but also to be more effective in your everyday life of school, art, sports and work. The author and movie producer Gotham Chopra, son of Deepak Chopra, told me that he absolutely must meditate for thirty minutes every day in order to be effective in his work and to maintain his inner peace.

Meditation is a time to be present and in the moment, and to pay attention to what you are feeling in your heart and in your body. Meditation can also be a valuable time to practice compassion toward other people and to remember our connection with the world around us. Meditation is crucial for anyone who is seeking to further their spiritual journey, as well as a great tool for making our day-to-day lives more peaceful and fulfilling.

Spiritual Activity #1
Breathe in your spirit.

Meditation is a discipline. Make your meditation practice as consistent as possible in order to experience its long-term benefits. Begin by sitting quietly on a chair or a mat with your back upright and your eyes closed for a short period of time—even five or ten minutes will be a good start. Concentrate on your breathing. Be aware of your breath coming in and out. Notice thoughts as they pass through your mind but then let them go and bring your awareness back to your breath.

Similarly, if a sound distracts you, let it go and bring your attention back to your breath. You can do a variation of this meditation even while sitting on the school bus or during a break at work.

If you want to further explore meditation, find a community of people to meditate with you. Like working out with a buddy can help you become a better athlete, meditating alongside others can help you to improve your practice. There are many different kinds of centers that offer forms of meditation, so feel free to visit several until you find the one that is right for you.

Spiritual Activity #2
Fill your heart.

Spend a part of each day thinking compassionate thoughts about people in your life—those you don't know, as well as those you do. Try to fill your heart with love and peace, even for people you don't get along with or who you have been told are "bad." Think of each person as just as valuable as you, no more or less. The Dalai Lama practices compassion in his meditation. "First, remember that we all want the same thing: to avoid suffering and find happiness," he said. "Second, begin each day with five minutes of compassionate breathing. Breathe in cherishing of the self; breathe out cherishing of others." The Dalai Lama's example allows you the valuable opportunity to exercise compassion for yourself as well as for other people.

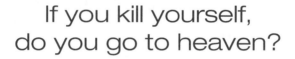

If you kill yourself, do you go to heaven?

Dear Pastor Paul,
If you kill yourself, do you go to heaven?

Dear Friend,

I take a strong stance against suicide because life is a precious gift and suicide is always a mistake and a tragedy. I also know that life will almost always get better if people can hold on until the pain and suffering diminish. However, I believe that people who kill themselves will be accepted and embraced in heaven. God will not offer double punishment for people who were already suffering so much on Earth, or to the families who may have lost a loved one to suicide. So if you are asking because a friend of yours killed himself or herself, I say that God is loving and all God's children are with God after death, including your friend.

If you are at all considering suicide as a possibility yourself—*stop*. Things *will* get better. Please look at this Web site that will give you a listing of suicide hotlines to call: *www.suicidehotlines .com/national.html*.

LIFE

LIFE IS THE FIRE THAT BURNS AND THE SUN THAT GIVES LIGHT.
LIFE IS THE WIND AND THE RAIN AND THE THUNDER IN THE SKY.
LIFE IS MATTER AND IS EARTH, WHAT IS AND WHAT IS NOT,
AND WHAT BEYOND IS IN ETERNITY.

Hindu

✦

NO MAN ENJOYS THE TRUE TASTE OF LIFE BUT HE
WHO IS READY AND WILLING TO QUIT IT.

Seneca

✦

THE UNEXAMINED LIFE IS NOT WORTH LIVING.

Socrates

LIFE IS REAL! LIFE IS EARNEST!
AND THE GRAVE IS NOT ITS GOAL;
DUST THOU ART, TO DUST RETURNEST,
WAS NOT SPOKEN OF THE SOUL.

Henry Wadsworth Longfellow

✦

LIFE IS LIKE MUSIC, IT MUST BE COMPOSED BY EAR,
FEELING AND INSTINCT, NOT BY RULE. NEVERTHELESS ONE HAD
BETTER KNOW THE RULES, FOR THEY SOMETIMES GUIDE IN
DOUBTFUL CASES, THOUGH NOT OFTEN.

Paracelsus

✦

A MORTAL LIVES NOT THROUGH THAT BREATH THAT
FLOWS IN AND THAT FLOWS OUT. THE SOURCE OF HIS LIFE IS
ANOTHER AND THIS CAUSES THE BREATH TO FLOW.

Kabbalah

✦

TWO ROADS DIVERGED IN A YELLOW WOOD, AND I—
I TOOK THE ONE LESS TRAVELED BY,
AND THAT HAS MADE ALL THE DIFFERENCE.

Robert Frost

How can I love myself if I feel so fat and helpless?

Dear Pastor Paul,

My friend says I can't love anyone else until I love myself first. I know I love other people, but I'm not sure I love myself. I'm not a skinny person like the world wants. When I get called fat, I get so upset. Every time I look in the mirror I see a fat, ugly, helpless girl, and I want to crawl up in a ball and die!!! I know God is there and will listen to me, but deep down I feel I've done too many things for him to really care about me. What can I do to get closer to God?

Dear Friend,

You are struggling with your own sense of self-worth. This is what your friend was talking about when she told you that you have to love yourself. Let me start by reassuring you that there is nothing that you can do to make God abandon you or not care about you. (Read Psalm 139 to know that God will never abandon you.)

I suggest you start by asking God for forgiveness for the things that cause you shame. God loves you completely and wants to help you to love yourself. God will cleanse you of your shame completely, if you ask.

If you feel your weight is out of control and you would like support, you may wish to look into Overeaters Anonymous, where you'll find supportive friends to help you to connect with a higher power (God) and overcome your eating problem. But your weight may not be the result of any problem at all. Remember that God made us all different sizes and shapes. God may have simply made you a little larger than others. If so, try to become comfortable in your body by focusing on the parts that you like. Be conscious of all the wonderful things that your body can do, such as walk and dance—and love.

PSALM 139

O LORD, YOU HAVE SEARCHED ME AND KNOWN ME.

YOU KNOW WHEN I SIT DOWN AND WHEN I RISE UP;

YOU DISCERN MY THOUGHTS FROM FAR AWAY.

YOU SEARCH OUT MY PATH AND MY LYING DOWN,

AND ARE ACQUAINTED WITH ALL MY WAYS.

EVEN BEFORE A WORD IS ON MY TONGUE, O LORD,

YOU KNOW IT COMPLETELY.

YOU HEM ME IN, BEHIND AND BEFORE,

AND LAY YOUR HAND UPON ME.

SUCH KNOWLEDGE IS TOO WONDERFUL FOR ME;

IT IS SO HIGH THAT I CANNOT ATTAIN IT.

WHERE CAN I GO FROM YOUR SPIRIT?

OR WHERE CAN I FLEE FROM YOUR PRESENCE?

IF I ASCEND TO HEAVEN, YOU ARE THERE;

IF I MAKE MY BED IN SHEOL, YOU ARE THERE.

IF I TAKE THE WINGS OF THE MORNING AND SETTLE

AT THE FARTHEST LIMITS OF THE SEA,

EVEN THERE YOUR HAND SHALL LEAD ME,

AND YOUR RIGHT HAND SHALL HOLD ME FAST.

IF I SAY, "SURELY THE DARKNESS SHALL COVER ME,

AND THE LIGHT AROUND ME BECOME NIGHT,"

EVEN THE DARKNESS IS NOT DARK TO YOU; THE NIGHT IS AS BRIGHT

AS THE DAY, FOR DARKNESS IS AS LIGHT TO YOU.

FOR IT WAS YOU WHO FORMED MY INWARD PARTS;

YOU KNIT ME TOGETHER IN MY MOTHER'S WOMB.

I PRAISE YOU, FOR I AM FEARFULLY AND WONDERFULLY MADE.

WONDERFUL ARE YOUR WORKS;

THAT I KNOW VERY WELL.

Why can't I hear God talking to me?

Dear Pastor Paul,

How do I know when I am talking to God? I am a sophomore in high school dealing with depression and low self-esteem. I don't have any friends. When I pray I ask God questions about how my life is going and why this stuff is happening to me. What did I do to deserve these things? I don't know if he's talking to me, or if it's my thoughts I'm hearing.

Dear Friend,

Your question is such a good one. Learning to distinguish our own will and thoughts from God's is a very subtle and profoundly important task.

Talking (or praying) to God is an intentional act different from having a running conversation in your head. You talk to God when you address God specifically and directly with your deepest love, hope and suffering. Make sure you pause to listen for God's response! In my experience, God doesn't blab on and on (unlike me sometimes), but instead offers a few words or even a feeling that truly changes my mind or soul. God's voice allows me to feel at peace and to know that my life will be all right. Even in my deepest struggles, when I hear God's voice I know that I'm loved. I encourage you to listen for this voice because, undoubtedly, God loves you too and is trying to communicate that to you.

I want to directly address your comment that you suffer from depression. Depression can be very serious. You should talk to your school counselor and make sure you see a mental-health professional in addition to any guidance you may already be getting from your pastor. Your life is precious, and you do not need to suffer alone. There are people who can help you. Let them.

HOPE

AT THE END OF THE DAY, WE MUST GO FORWARD WITH
HOPE AND NOT BACKWARD BY FEAR AND DIVISION.

Rev. Jesse Jackson

✦

WE SUFFER FROM AN INCURABLE MALADY: HOPE

Mahmoud Darwish, Palestinian poet

✦

YOUTHS MAY FAINT AND BE WEARY, AND YOUNG
MEN MAY FALL, EXHAUSTED; BUT THEY WHO HOPE IN THE LORD
SHALL RENEW THEIR STRENGTH. THEY SHALL MOUNT UP
WITH WINGS LIKE EAGLES, THEY SHALL RUN AND NOT BE WEARY,
THEY SHALL WALK AND NOT GROW FAINT.

Isaiah 40:28–31

✦

IF GOD GIVES YOU A CUP OF WINE AND AN EVIL-MINDED
PERSON KICKS IT OVER, HE FILLS IT UP FOR YOU AGAIN.

African Proverb (Ghana)

What should I do with my life?

Dear Pastor Paul,

Help! I don't know what I am supposed to do with my life! I am a freshman in college and part of going to college is deciding on the career that we are going to have. While that seems to be easy for some people (like my roommate, who seems to have everything mapped out), I am still completely undecided. All I know is that I want to be happy, and I want to serve God in the best way I can. Any ideas for a career?

Dear Friend,

What you are looking for is not just a job, but a vocation, or a calling. A vocation is different from a job. A job is something you do primarily to get money. A vocation combines your unique gifts and talents with a need in the world. It connects your life to the wider purpose God has for the universe.

I believe we all have a vocation. For some, it means volunteering—coaching soccer for kids after school or organizing a yearly food drive for the poor. For others, it means teaching; for others, it can mean being a lawyer. For me, it means being a minister.

Make a list of activities you enjoy doing and relate them to your talents. Make another list of what you feel the world needs, such as a cleaner environment, less hunger, more beautiful art, more belief in religion—whatever is important to you. Keep adding to these lists, and at some point you will see where your talents and the world's needs come together to form your vocation. One last thing —you don't have to decide this right away. What's more, you can reassess your vocation throughout your life. Just know that God does have a use for your life, so keep looking.

Spiritual **Journaling**

Journaling is like keeping a diary, only with more focus and what's known in spiritual circles as "intention." Journaling provides the opportunity to reflect on the people you meet, the places you go and the things you do. In the simple act of writing you can see the sacredness of your life. Writing in your journal will help you recognize that your life is not merely a series of coincidences but has an underlying purpose. Writing in your journal will help you to find that purpose. In a way, writing your spiritual journal is like writing an ongoing spiritual autobiography.

The sacred texts of the world's religions record how the Divine worked in the lives of famous figures such as Jesus, Moses, Muhammad, Buddha, etc. The stories in those sacred texts are not unlike your own story if you believe that the Sacred is still alive and well in the world and working in your life. Spiritual journaling will give you the opportunity to reflect on how your spiritual life is progressing and ways to live it out in the world.

Spiritual Activity #1
Detailing the spiritual.

A blank book is best for spiritual journaling, but yellow pads or other notebooks are just fine. Set aside at least ten minutes before bed to record the events of the day, including moments of prayer, meditation or service. Pay attention to any new people you meet and what they might mean for your life—remember, spiritual guides come in all ages, colors, shapes and sizes. Reflect on opportunities and challenges you are facing. Why are they coming into your life right now? What could be the opportunity for spiritual growth you can learn from these people and events? Cut out pictures, scripture or quotes that have spiritual value to you and tape them into your journal. Write about why that particular image or quote has value. Take time to read over your journal at the end of each week. Note any spiritual breakthroughs as well as challenges that you would like to address in the coming week.

Spiritual Activity #2
Spiritual brainstorming.

Try setting categories for yourself and see how you can fill them in.

Start by brainstorming categories you believe constitute a full spiritual life. Some might be "prayer," "service," "peace" or "joy." As you write in your journal, observe how often your life is filling these categories. This may offer you insight into how you are presently living your life and goals for how you would like to live your life in the future. You may wish to set a spiritual goal for yourself. An example would be "To have more peace by the end of the year." Use your journal to reflect upon your specific work toward that goal, both in your spiritual life and in the world.

Spiritual Activity #3
Writing to God.

Use your journaling time to converse with the Divine within you. Write a question that is important to you, such as, "What am I meant to do with my life?" Or, "Why is there sadness or death in the world?" Next, take a different color pen and write whatever answer spontaneously comes to mind. You may be surprised by the sacred wisdom within you that is waiting to be expressed.

CHAPTER 9

LOSING & FINDING YOUR RELIGION

Where was God on 9/11?

Dear Pastor Paul,

I am having a rough time with my faith in light of the attacks on America. I have tried to turn to prayer for comfort, but there are nagging questions left in my mind. Why did this happen? Why did God allow for such terrible evil to happen? Where was he?

Dear Friend,

Your question boils the attacks down to fundamental questions about the omnipotence (all powerfulness) and benevolence (complete goodness) of God. We all ask these questions when we are touched by suffering and death. I struggled with these questions when I was a chaplain in a hospital and saw patients I loved and knew to be good people suffer and die. I continue to struggle with these questions as I also recover from the attacks.

Suffering and evil do exist in this world. God is not in the evil. God did not promote or participate in any way in these attacks, any more than God participated in the cancer that killed my beloved patients in the hospital. God is in the response to the evil—which can prevent further evil. God is all-powerful insofar as we are willing to receive God's grace in transforming evil into good and suffering into compassion.

Continue to pray. You can be angry at God, you can be sorrowful with God. Ultimately, instead of asking God for answers to why, which do not lead to truth, but only human rationalization, ask how. How can we be agents of God's grace in the world that is filled with evils such as war, starvation, violence and hate? How can we be the touch of compassion in the face of suffering? How can God's will be done through us? Through these acts, we will begin to feel God's presence in the world and perhaps understand the Divine in a deeper way than we thought possible. People will point to the work we are doing and say, "Look how God is working in the world. Look how the kingdom of God is being built from the ashes."

CELEBRITY SPIRITUALITY

"In the ancient kabbalistic and Talmudic writings, there are references made to the idea that before Adam, there was primordial man, and energy—spirituality—exuded from his eyes. The energy, the spirituality, was to be caught in vessels to be distributed through the universe.

"But there was too much energy for the vessels to contain, they broke, and this spirituality was scattered throughout the universe in shards. The task of humanity is to collect those shards by the doing of positive and good deeds. When they are all back together again, the universe will be healed.

"I'm touched by the idea that when we do things that are useful and helpful—collecting these shards of spirituality—that we may be helping to bring about a healing."

Q: Are you referring to the concept of Tikkun?

"Yes, exactly. The healing of the world, the healing of the universe."

Leonard Nimoy in the *Beliefnet* interview by Anne Simpkinson

Can I get "hard evidence" to help me believe?

Dear Pastor,

I've been going to a Christian school all my life, but recently I feel I need "hard evidence" to believe, and Christianity is based on faith, right? The burning question of whether all of this is true is separating me from Jesus. What can I do to get this off my mind?

Dear Friend,

You have brought up an essential element of religion: belief. Belief, or faith, is what makes religion different from science. Science requires that things be repeatedly consistent in their behavior and verifiable to all. Belief is based on experience, feelings and intuition of individuals, and the testimonies of these individuals passed down from generation to generation. Both are considered paths to an understanding of the truth.

Whether what you believe is true or not depends on the value that you place on your own feelings and experiences, and those of Christians who have come before you. If you have loved Jesus and have experienced God in your life, then that is "hard evidence" and absolutely true.

CELEBRITY SPIRITUALITY

"I grew up Presbyterian, just a basic Protestant upbringing. There were years in my life when I would go to church every Sunday and to Sunday school. Then I just phased out of it. I believed in God my whole life, and then strayed away from it in my teenage years, until recently.

"Luckily, I always maintained a dialogue with God, especially in my darkest hours. You know, it is like that Footprints poem. It really is like that for me. When I was at my worst—I really am trying not to cry right now—I was really in contact with God, just praying with conviction to just please get me out of this."

Andy Dick in the *Beliefnet* interview by Steven Lawson

Why I'm Sikh

by Mallika Kaur

Being a Sikh is a choice.

This idea was alien to me for the first eighteen years of my life.

My parents were Sikhs, and so that made me a Sikh too, right? This easy understanding was questioned when I came to college. When I was questioned as to what my religion was, I began to realize I didn't have answers.

I had never been a spiritual person, in fact, quite the contrary; I could never understand what it meant to be "touched by grace." It was in a room full of sixty kids that I was touched. It was at a Sikh kids' camp, where I sat in the prayer room and listened to kids half my age sing *shabads* (sacred hymns).

My friends had always known me as "dry-eyes," but sitting in this room, listening to the *shabads* and feeling the genuine effort and faith, tears streamed down my face. It was such an unusual feeling that I just wiped the first few away and went outside. I sat in the grass and stared at the tall trees in front of me and wondered if I was going crazy! I could not stop crying. I had always talked to some higher power at night before going to sleep. But this time it was different. I kept saying in my head, "Help me stop crying," and that just brought more tears. Something had changed inside me. I had developed a "thirst."

Being a Sikh is a way of life.

JUST THE FAQs SIKHISM

- A person who follows the religion called Sikhism is a Sikh.

- Sikhs worship in a Gurdwara.

- A Sikh religious leader or teacher is called granthi.

- The primary sacred writing is called Guru Granth Sahib.

- Age: Approximately 500 years

- Country of origin: Punjab, India

- Number of American Sikhs: 60,000

- Number of Sikhs worldwide: 23 million

The thirst I developed made me want to understand the nature of my faith more and also try to figure out what it was that brought me closer to Waheguru (the Sikh word for the Omnipotent One). I discovered that the Sikh idea of *seva* (community service) was what gave me the most joy. I started working with a number of volunteer organizations, like Chicago Cares and the Sikh Coalition, to help others. I also began training to volunteer with a Chicago nonprofit called Rape Victim Advocates. I take shifts every month and get called to the emergency room when a rape victim is brought in and help them with legal, medical and emotional issues. My faith gives me strength to face the sadness, frustration and rage one encounters in this work. I come home and remember Waheguru and count all my blessings.

Sikhs believe that one can achieve that ultimate state of "oneness" through all paths that promote love, and this makes me respect all people's journeys. Being interested in my faith brings me closer to other people; some whom I volunteer with, some whom I volunteer to help, some friends and others whom I admire for having the conviction to stick to their faith.

Being a Sikh gives me thirst, but also a lot of happiness and a lot of friends!

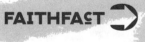

FAITHFACT Attaining wisdom is an essential life goal for 86% of college students in the USA, while becoming a more loving person is an essential life goal for 84%.

Is it okay to read religious texts other than my own?

Dear Pastor Paul,

I am a Protestant, and I believe in God, but I also like to read other religions' texts in order to get a better understanding of that religion. I'm told that Buddhist writings might have a lot to say to me, since I am a pacifist. Is it okay to read other texts and incorporate basic moral beliefs from other religions and philosophies into everyday life, still holding true to my own religion?

Dear Friend,

Not only is it okay to read sacred texts other than your own, I think it's very important to do so. Knowing some of the basic beliefs and wisdom of other religions makes you better able to love and respect your neighbors who practice those faiths. Each of us should go as deep into our own religious traditions as we are capable, and I hope you will continue to practice your Christian faith and learn all the richness that Christianity holds. But in looking at other religious texts, you'll absorb some wonderful spiritual principles that may help you along the way.

For instance, the Buddha has many sayings about peace and compassion. If you do read Buddhist texts, I suspect you'll be interested to see the similarities between the Buddha's and Jesus' teachings about peace. To read specifically about the intersections of Buddhism and Christianity, you may wish to pick up a book by Vietnamese Buddhist monk Thich Nhat Hanh called *Living Buddha, Living Christ.*

WISDOM

When you reach the end of what you should know,
you will be at the beginning of what
you should sense.

Kahlil Gibran

◆

Imagination is more important
than knowledge.

Albert Einstein

◆

The Master said, "A gentleman can see a question from
all sides without bias. The small man is biased and
can see a question only from one side."

Confucianism

◆

As the heat of a fire reduces wood to ashes,
the fire of knowledge burns to ashes all karma.
Nothing in this world purifies like spiritual wisdom.
It is the perfection achieved in time through the path of yoga,
the path which leads to the Self within.

Hinduism

THOSE WHO SEE TRUTH AND SPEAK TRUTH,
THEIR BODIES AND MINDS BECOME TRUTHFUL.
TRUTH IS THEIR EVIDENCE, TRUTH IS THEIR INSTRUCTION,
TRUE IS THE PRAISE OF THE TRUTHFUL.
THOSE WHO HAVE FORGOTTEN TRUTH CRY IN AGONY
AND WEEP WHILE DEPARTING.

Sikhism

✦

HE WHO KNOWS OTHERS IS LEARNED.
HE WHO KNOWS HIMSELF IS WISE.

Taoism

✦

THE SEARCH FOR KNOWLEDGE IS AN OBLIGATION
LAID ON EVERY MUSLIM.

Islam

Can I be a Christian and practice yoga?

Dear Pastor Paul,

I am a Christian who has recently been researching yoga. I read that yoga is not part of the Hindu religion, but is meant to bring you closer to God. I'm wondering if there are any contradictions between yoga and my beliefs. Could you possibly inform me of anything that might not agree? Thank you and God bless.

Dear Friend,

The founders of *hatha* yoga (which is the kind with different poses you are most probably studying) were indeed the same people who developed the philosophies of Hinduism. In fact, yoga means union with God and is practiced in many different forms in Hinduism. However, in recent years *hatha* yoga has become largely disassociated from its religious moorings and is practiced by people of all beliefs, as often for its purely physical benefits as for its spiritual ones.

There are yoga teachers who teach from the Christian perspective. I recently took a class like this on a church retreat. It's a beautiful mix and was very peaceful, and it gave me an incarnate sense of the Divine. Ultimately, it's up to you to decide if the modern practice of yoga contradicts your Christian beliefs. You may be of a tradition that doesn't allow any influences that are not from the Christian faith. But many people find that yoga brings them closer to God and that the poses help them to meditate on the Divine—Christians and Hindus alike.

Can you practice yoga and not be Hindu?

Dear Pastor Paul,

In a recent column, your answer to a reader about practicing yoga made it appear that you sanction the way the West has divorced the many varieties of yoga from the religion of Hinduism. If so, let us talk about that. Brahman bless.

Dear Friend,

The letter you saw was from a Christian who wondered if practicing yoga was against her faith. In the West, the word "yoga" has come to mean a form of exercise based on poses (*asanas*) derived from *hatha* yoga. It is used for meditation and to promote physical well-being. I told her that yoga is not dangerous to Christians and can help people of all religions "unite with God."

I appreciate that practicing Hinduism isn't the same as taking a yoga class at a gym, or even that taking a class exposes the student to all levels of spiritual discipline yoga offers. I understand from your letter that you'd like people to explore more deeply the spiritual discipline of yoga and to understand the wider framework of the Hindu religion.

While it's frustrating for orthodox religious practitioners, some spiritual disciplines created within religions take on a life of their own. Sufism was born of Islam, and Kabbalah comes out of Judaism; both of these spiritual practices have students who are not Muslim or Jewish but for whom these particular paths have nonetheless been immensely helpful.

Yoga has become a spiritual discipline that, like it or not, has reached beyond its original Hindu context. If a Christian, even someone far removed from the great centers of Hinduism in India, experiences a blissful moment of mindfulness and peace in a yoga class, I am all for it. My guess is that the many Yogi masters might agree.

CELEBRITY SPIRITUALITY

"I started practicing yoga at about eighteen. I had a friend who was doing it and was incredibly disciplined and meditated all the time. I found it really intriguing. I think yoga was the thing that attracted me to this friend in the first place. It was sort of like, *wow*, the discipline and the respect and the quietude.

"That's what I wanted. I started to do *kundalini* yoga, which is not the yoga I do now, but it's a yoga that I believe originated with the Sikhs, who combined Islamic and Hindu practices. It's based a little on meditation, but there is a physical aspect to the practice, too.

"I did it quite regularly. I had a daily meditation practice and started to go to retreats from time to time. But at the time I was traveling and working a lot as a model. I used some of the tools that I learned through meditation and yoga to keep me calm and sane through my career. I didn't always have an *asana* practice, but I continued to use things such as meditation, mantra repetition and breathing exercises to keep me balanced and centered."

Christy Turlington in the *Beliefnet* interview by Anne Simpkinson

What The Religions Say About MYSTICISM

All five major religions have an esoteric, or obscure, strain called mysticism. Those who practice mysticism concern themselves with the secret wisdom about the nature of the universe that underlies their faith. Mystics are also committed to experiencing union with God during this life. While the mystics are sometimes viewed with suspicion by people who believe in strict observance of the laws of their own religion, they often report direct, personal experiences of God and claim wisdom about the nature of the universe that crosses religious boundaries.

Buddhism—Meditation

Buddhism is not a theistic religion like Christianity, Judaism, Islam or even Hinduism, so Buddhists do not have the goal of merging the self with God. However, Buddhism is meant to be a technique for losing the individual self, dualism and material attachments into the wider reality. Buddhists believe that once an individual has achieved the extinction of all distinctions, or all words, concepts and ideas, they have reached the state of *nirvana*. Buddhists work toward the goal of *nirvana* through meditation and mindfulness.

As this quote from the Buddhist text *Sutta Nipata* shows, the goal of Buddhist meditation and mindfulness is to let go of attachment to the self and feel at one with the universe, similar to the goal of union with God in other mystical traditions:

"As in the ocean's midmost depth no wave is born, but all is still, so let the practitioner be still, be motionless, and nowhere should one swell."

Christianity—Mysticism

Christian mystics have been around throughout the history of the Christian church. They include the early desert fathers and monks and nuns throughout the ages who dedicated their lives to contemplative prayer and communion with God. Teresa of Avila, Catherine of Siena and Juliana of Norwich were some of the most famous women Christian mystics who lived in the Middle Ages and who sometimes spoke of Jesus almost as a husband and lover. Today Christian mystics can be found among laypeople throughout Christianity such as in the ecumenical Roman Catholic Taize services; the Quakers, who feel that God speaks to them through their inner voices; and Pentecostals, who experience God manifest through the Holy Spirit in their worship services.

What makes all of Christian mystics similar is an experiential knowledge of Jesus and a burning passion to join their own lives with God. As the mystic Meister Eckhart said, "God guides the redeemed through a narrow way into the broad road, so that they come into the wide and broad place; that is to say, into true freedom of the spirit, when one has become a spirit with God."

Hinduism—Yoga

Although many Americans have started taking yoga at the local gym, yoga is more than an alternative to a step class or lifting weights. In fact, the word "yoga" in Hinduism means "union" or the "mystical joining with God." The aim of the Hindu is to merge his or her own soul, or *atman*, entirely with Brahman, or the absolute truth underlying reality of the universe or God. In order to accomplish this, Hindus practice distinct forms of yoga, each corresponding to a different approach to connecting with God.

Hinduism's first ambassador to American shores, Swami Vivekananda, summarized these different approaches as the four yogas: *karma* yoga (performing good deeds and activism for God); *bhakti* yoga (filled with love and devotion toward God); *jnana* yoga (the intellectual pursuit of knowledge of God); and *raja* yoga (the holistic approach to God that includes mind, body and spirit). *Hatha* yoga is one of the physical parts of *raja* yoga that has become very popular in the United States. When practiced with attention and discipline, each one of these yogas can lead to a union with God.

The man of yoga who is able
to overcome, here on earth,
the turmoil of desire and anger—
that man is truly happy.
He who finds peace and joy
and radiance within himself—
that man becomes one with God
And vanishes into God's bliss.

Bhagavad Gita
(Translation by Stephen Mitchell)

Islam—Sufism

Sufism is the mystical branch of Islam. It is practiced all around the world by a diverse group of people known as Sufis. The name Sufi originally comes from the word *suf,* which means "wool" because the earliest practitioners wore woolen garments as protest against the worldliness of the rulers who wore satin and silk. From *suf* comes the Arabic term *tasawwuf,* or mysticism. Sufis are interested in the deep universal spiritual messages of Islam and attaining complete union with God in this life. Sufis believe that it is possible to become close to God and to experience this closeness—while one is alive.

In the Sufi tradition you must have a teacher (*sheikh*) because Sufi wisdom is handed down through a succession of teachers. To be a Sufi it's necessary to go through a ceremony in which you "take hand"—announcing that you are following a certain *sheikh*. Sufis often use dance, music and chanting in the quest to come closer to God, but Sufism has especially offered the world wonderful spiritual poetry. In fact, one of the most popular poets in America is

Rumi, the thirteenth-century Turkish mystic who wrote:

If you could get rid
of yourself just once,
The secret of secrets
Would open to you.
The face of the unknown,
Hidden beyond the universe
Would appear on the
Mirror of your perception.

Judaism—The Kabbalah

Although Madonna has made it popular in the last years, Kabbalah, the Jewish mystical tradition, is not a recent phenomenon—it goes back to the Torah. Kabbalists believe the Torah holds an underlying wisdom that, when read in a particular way, will lead to mystical revelation about the nature of God's working in the universe and in the human soul. Kabbalah is Hebrew for the word "received" because practitioners of Kabbalah originally received their knowledge orally from teacher to student. The *Zohar* (Hebrew for "illuminated") is the main text of the Kabbalah and is a mystical commentary on the Torah. The text appeared in Spain in the 1300s, but many believe that it was written in the second century.

Tradition used to hold that one must reach the age of forty before beginning to explore Kabbalah because younger people were not considered to have the necessary background or emotional maturity to be able to deal with the topic. That is not equally true today, as many younger people explore Kabbalah study, but many still feel that this practice should not be approached lightly.

In Kabbalah, each letter of the Torah has an underlying significance. God is called *Ein Sof*, which in Hebrew means "without end." Ein Sof interacts with the world through the interconnecting, diverse energies of God known as *Sefirot*. These energies are: crown, wisdom, understanding, kindness, strength, beauty, victory, awe, foundation and manifestation, or God's presence in the world.

The kabbalist and former chief rabbi of Palestine in the days before the state of Israel was founded, Abraham Isaac Kook, wrote this poem, which shows some of the power of the Kabbalah:

Within our souls lights divine arise
In multiform shapes, according to our
    minds.
The One, Eternal Truth,
Before the One,
In depths of Holy Truth,
Revealed is He.
Within us dominant,
Ruling our inner soul,
The soul of all creation.

Can I believe in evolution and keep my faith?

Dear Pastor Paul,

I was raised a Southern Baptist. Lately I have been doing a lot of reading in scientific books, and they have made me a firm believer in evolution. How can I believe in evolution and still keep my faith?

Dear Friend,

Being a person of faith doesn't mean you have to disregard scientific knowledge. Albert Einstein was not a very religious man, but he wrote: "A legitimate conflict between science and religion cannot exist. Science without religion is lame, religion without science is blind." I believe in the basic principles and time frame of evolution, yet I still believe God exists and has influenced the entire process.

My advice to you is to develop your own synthesis of knowledge from what the Bible says and what you read in science. Consider science a method of carefully examining the world that God created. Look to the Bible to understand how God touches human lives and as an invitation to personally experience God today. Keep studying while you keep praying and going to church, and you should have no difficulty keeping your faith.

CELEBRITY SPIRITUALITY

> "I trust the Hindu belief Nada Brahma, or God is sound. The universe started in a vibration, and that first sound is still washing over us. That's the old Hindu belief. It's the origin of the universe theory: The universe started an arrhythmic event. The Big Bang occurred, and there was another sound after that, and that was the first rhythm. I talk about it in my book. So I'd have to believe that's my cosmology."
>
> Mickey Hart from the Grateful Dead in the *Beliefnet* interview by Paul Raushenbush

Is faith overrated?

Dear Pastor Paul,

Is faith overrated? Does it mean doing everything right, as he told us to? Can one have faith and question the Bible as a true inspiration from God?

Dear Friend,

Faith is only overrated if it has been ill-defined. Does faith mean not doubting anything ever again? No. Will it make you perfect or make your problems go away? No. If these are your expectations of a faithful life, then, yes, faith is overrated.

That said, the gift from God of faith in God was the greatest event of my life. That faith gives me the opportunity to feel a sense of unity and intimacy with God and the whole of humanity. I no longer feel alone. Faith in the power of God gives me the ability to depend upon this power to help me overcome the struggles I continue to face. Faith is a basic stance of positivity. "Have faith" is an urging to believe that things will work out for the best, even when they look their worst. Do not forget that faith is a two-way street. Once you establish faith with God, God has faith in you. God's gift of faith gives us confidence to live life with a sense of purpose and meaning. Through faith, God trusts us to be a divine presence in the world.

I pray that you will enjoy the wonders of faith in your life.

Inspiring **Religious Heroes**

Pastor Paul's Tips for Spiritual Seekers

All of us have heroines and heroes whose personal lives provide us with inspiration and examples as to how to live our own lives. These folks can be our parents, famous athletes, politicians, or film or music stars. Choosing spiritual and authentic religious people to be your heroes can inspire you to live your own life with religious conviction and courage. Remember, you have as many seconds in a minute, minutes in an hour and hours in a day as your heroine or hero. Use your life well, and you may be a spiritual hero for the next generation.

Spiritual Activity #1
Find your religious hero.

Decide on an important historical religious figure as your role model. Some examples might be Mahatma Gandhi, the Dalai Lama, Mother Teresa, Golda Meir, Black Elk or Muhammad Ali. Read a biography of their life, noting the experiences they have had in their lives: What was their childhood like? What difficulties did they have to overcome? Who and what were the driving forces in their lives? How did they become religious, and what kind of daily religious observance did they make? What can you learn from their example?

Spiritual Activity #2
A hero close to home.

Identify someone you know well whose religious commitment you admire. This can be your local priest, rabbi, imam, or even your grandmother or uncle. Ask them if they would meet with you for an interview. You may wish to ask them the questions from spiritual activity #1, or come up with your own list. Ask them if they would be willing to have you mirror them, or follow them around for a day to see what goes into a day of religious commitment like your religious hero.

Spiritual Activity #3
Look beyond your horizons . . .

Read about several important religious people outside of your own tradition. Identify some universal characteristics that all people with religious commitment share, such as overcoming difficult circumstances, sacrifice, integrity, selflessness, compassion and discipline. Cultivate these characteristics in yourself through your daily activities.

Does God love the poor or the rich more?

Dear Pastor Paul,

I read that Mahatma Gandhi said that the poor were the children of God, and Jesus also talks about how the poor will inherit the Earth—but if that is true, then why do they suffer? It seems like God loves the rich more.

Dear Friend,

God loves all people equally. However, many of the sacred texts of the world's religions do emphasize God's special empathy for those who are weak, poor and humble, and they also stress God's clear intolerance of humankind's complacency in the face of poverty. The rich can run the risk of believing they are self-sufficient because of their wealth. It can be tempting to focus one's attention on money and getting more, and less on God.

The poor, by contrast, don't have the protection of luxury. They see how dependent we are on God on a firsthand basis. In my tradition, Jesus preached about the coming of the kingdom of God, when all would have enough to eat and nobody would be desperately poor. The kingdom of God calls for reconciliation and inclusion of all God's children—both rich and poor.

JUST THE FAQS
BAHA'I

- A person who practices the Baha'i faith is a Baha'i.

- Major Branches: The Baha'i World Faith.

- The founder of the Baha'i faith is Bab and Baha'u'llah.

- Baha'is worship in a center.

- There is no separate clergy class.

- The primary sacred writings are the writings of the Bab and Baha'u'llah.

- Age: 160 years

- Country of origin: Persia, now Iran

- Number of American Baha'is: 90,000

- Number of Baha'is worldwide: 6 million

Why I'm Baha'i

by Michelle Hemmat

When I was a child, the Baha'i faith was a precious gift presented lovingly to me by my family. It was the prayers they taught me, the stories they told and the songs they sang. I fell in love with the Baha'i faith at an early age. With that love came the responsibility to undertake the challenge that the faith presented—to live an upright life shaped around the goal of serving humanity. Although fulfilling this is a personal journey, many of the growth spurts that I experienced were through participation in the activities of the Baha'i community.

During the years of middle school and high school, I participated in the Baha'i Youth Workshop, a performing arts group that addressed social issues such as racism, sexism and substance abuse through dance, rap and theater. We met every Sunday not only to rehearse, but also to study the Baha'i writings, discuss the challenges that we confronted in our everyday lives, and provide support for each other. As Baha'i youth, our mission was to uphold a rectitude of conduct that caused all our actions to ring with justice, honesty, kindness and trustworthiness. Our thoughts and actions were to maintain a standard of chastity and purity that must contrast starkly with those of our peers. We also sought to actively battle the cancer of racial prejudice that ate away at our society. Underlying all of these principles was an emphasis on the importance of service to our community. We focused on achieving these goals in our lives and portrayed them through our performances at high schools, juvenile detention centers, as well as community events following race riots that occurred in a nearby town. My participation in the Baha'i Youth Workshop allowed me to experience at an early age the rewards and challenges of attempting to create positive changes in my community. The support of my fellow Baha'i youth gave me strength to be different from my teenage peers, who were prone to become involved in unhealthy pastimes and habits.

I have received the same gifts and lessons that I gained from the Baha'i Youth Workshop in many different forms as I moved to different towns and participated in different kinds of Baha'i activities. In Venezuela, I worked on a Baha'i project focused on moral education of children and took part in new methods of studying the Baha'i writings in groups. In college, I attended Baha'i conferences on social and economic development. In all these activities, the Baha'is provided me with enthusiasm and support in undertaking the responsibilities that my love for the faith impressed upon me.

Pastor Paul's Tips for Spiritual Seekers

Service

Community service is part of many school curricula these days, but it's not always taught as a spiritual activity. Yet the act of helping others can be the single most effective way to advance on your spiritual path. All religious traditions strongly emphasize service and charity as an integral part of what it means to be spiritual. In Islam, service or charity is called *zakaah*; in Judaism it is called *g'milut chasadim*, or acts of loving-kindness; and in Hinduism and Sikhism it is *seva*. You can't consider yourself a follower of these religions without doing some kind of service; it's that important.

Service is also an enormous relief from the incessant striving in our culture, where getting ahead is a priority. When you serve others you connect your spirit to the spirit of your fellow human beings. When we are engaged in service we are not out for material gain, or to be impressive in other people's eyes. Rather we are performing the pure spiritual practice of giving and doing unto others as you would have them do unto you. As the musician Ben Harper put it, "When you get there (heaven's gates) they don't ask you what you saved, all they want to know is what you gave." ("Excuse Me, Mr." from *Fight for Your Mind*.)

Spiritual Activity #1
Commit to service!

If you're not involved in a service activity already, commit to a project that interests you, such as a soup kitchen, a clothing bank, house building or helping out in a senior citizens' home. Stay with it for at least six months so you get to know some of the people you are serving. Don't be afraid to talk or, better yet, listen. Sometimes the stories of those you serve are amazingly diverse and not at all what you might have expected from someone in need. You may hear stories about families and jobs that the people in the shelter maintain, even though they don't have a permanent home. Make sure any volunteer work you do starts with a good orientation so you will have the opportunity to ask any questions you might have.

Spiritual Activity #2
Make the connection.

If you already perform some service, make the connection between service and the sacred by finding quotes from your sacred texts. Post them in your room to inspire you, or reflect on these with your youth group or friends.

Spiritual Activity #3
More to give . . .

You may also want to back up your gift of time by giving your own money to a charity. Don't discount the amount you're able to offer. You can save a child from dying of starvation for a month for the price of a couple of movies. Take part in a fundraiser for an organization you believe in. AIDS organizations, MS and cancer societies and associations all have bike rides and walks that raise money for these important groups. Reflecting on how you are using your resources is a spiritual discipline.

What if I think church is lame?

Dear Pastor Paul,

Recently I have not been wanting to go to church, not because I don't think I should, but I don't really get anything out of it. What do you think I should do?

Dear Friend,

The truth is that all churches are not created equal. Go find a faith community that inspires and nurtures you and your relationship with God. Visiting churches can be fun. The church for you is out there—keep looking.

CELEBRITY SPIRITUALITY

"I'm thinking maybe religion is the problem. Because religion is man-made. It's a man who said, 'Okay, you should go to this church every Sunday, you should go to the Kingdom Hall and go out to field service, you should go to the mosque. You should do all these things, this is what you should do.' Who told you? In the Bible God said to come as you are. Who made these laws, that's what I want to know. So that's why I wear two crosses now. I call it double cross. I believe in God and not religion, because I believe religion is the double-cross. Because I've been double-crossed by three religions, so I think I can safely say that religion—there is maybe something wrong with religion. Every temple that's put up may not be a holy one, so watch out."

Ja Rule in the *Beliefnet* interview by Paul Raushenbush

Religions cause war, so why be religious?

Dear Pastor Paul,

Why should anyone be religious when so many of the wars and prejudice have been based on religion?

Dear Friend,

Of course I am biased, but I believe that religion is a good thing. Religion can be used to create prejudice and division, but then, so can race or nationality. Like race and nationality, our religion is one of the things that makes us who we are.

Wars and prejudice are started because of fear, greed and ignorance. Those are the real troubles, not religion. My suggestion is for all of us to try to meet someone who practices a faith different from our own, get to know them as people and friends and to learn about their beliefs. When we know someone of another faith personally, we are less likely to view any one religion as "bad" or the "enemy."

Every religion has some version of the golden rule of treating others as you would like to be treated, and I suggest we use that as our common ground.

THE GOLDEN RULE

WHAT IS HATEFUL TO YOU, DO NOT TO YOUR FELLOW MEN.
THAT IS THE ENTIRE LAW, ALL THE REST IS COMMENTARY.

Judaism

AS YE WOULD THAT MEN SHOULD DO TO YOU,
DO YE ALSO TO THEM LIKEWISE.

Christianity

NOT ONE OF YOU IS A BELIEVER UNTIL HE LOVES FOR
HIS BROTHER WHAT HE LOVES FOR HIMSELF.

Islam

IF IT HARM NO ONE, DO WHAT THOU WILT
[I.E., DO WHATEVER YOU WANT, AS LONG AS IT HARMS
NOBODY, INCLUDING YOURSELF].

The Wiccan Rede

I AM GOOD TO THE MAN WHO IS GOOD TO ME, LIKEWISE,
I AM ALSO GOOD TO THE BAD MAN.

Tao Te Ching

THE HEART OF THE PERSON BEFORE YOU IS A MIRROR.
SEE THERE YOUR OWN FORM.

Shintoism

✦

TSEKUNG ASKED, "IS THERE ONE WORD THAT CAN
SERVE AS A PRINCIPLE OF CONDUCT FOR LIFE?" CONFUCIUS REPLIED,
"IT IS THE WORD SHU—RECIPROCITY: DO NOT DO TO OTHERS
WHAT YOU DO NOT WANT THEM TO DO TO YOU."

Confucianism

✦

ONE GOING TO TAKE A POINTED STICK TO PINCH A BABY BIRD
SHOULD FIRST TRY IT ON HIMSELF TO FEEL HOW IT HURTS.

African Yoruba Proverb

INTERFAITH FOCUS:
FACE TO FACE/
FAITH TO FAITH

FACE TO FACE/FAITH TO FAITH IS AN organization that advances a groundbreaking strategy for peaceful coexistence. Its mission is to equip the next generation of young leaders with an advanced understanding of how their own religious traditions (and those of others) can be used to build a more peaceful and just world. Based in New York, there are currently fifty teen members, ages sixteen to eighteen, from Northern Ireland, South Africa, the Middle East and the U.S.—Jews, Christians and Muslims—who come together for a summer workshop program. Drawing upon established principles of communication skills-building, multifaith education, youth development and conflict management, Face to Face provides a forum for sustained interaction, dialogue and collaboration among young people of diverse religious, ethnic, racial and socioeconomic backgrounds whose communities are divided by faith, identity and culture.

Face to Face/Faith to Faith, by Hannah Ellenson

Before this past summer I had never even met, let alone befriended, a Muslim. Having grown up in a Jewish family with two rabbis as parents, I have not been exposed to much beyond the vibrant Jewish communities that existed in Los Angeles, Jerusalem and now New York. But last summer at an interfaith coexistence program, Face to Face/Faith to Faith, my best friends were Christians, Jews, Muslims and Hindus from Northern Ireland, Israel and South Africa. Never had I lived, worked and played in such a diverse environment where each person's opinions and experiences could not have differed more from the next.

During the program, all fifty of us took a trip into New York City for a few days. We stayed in the basement of my synagogue, which was only two blocks from my house. While there, we were going to be without showers for two days. For most of us, this was not such a problem. But for others, this posed a huge dilemma. Muslims, before they pray, must be "pure." Islamic tradition understands this to mean that Muslims must wash their entire body before they offer their morning prayers. The nearest accessible shower was at my house. Since the camp director knew this, she asked me if they could come to my house before sunrise to cleanse themselves and pray. Without the slightest hesitation, I immediately said yes.

The next morning, we woke up at 4:30 a.m. so everyone could shower and pray before sunrise. While I waited for everybody to come out of the room, one of the boys, Omar, walked out sleepily wearing a shirt that proclaimed in big, bold letters "Free Palestine." I love Israel, and while I am in favor of a two-state solution to the Israeli-Palestinian conflict, I was uncomfortable with someone in my house wearing something that I found so blatantly offensive. Omar's shirt implied that Israel must be destroyed. I realized there was a limit to my liberalism. As comfortable as I was having my new friends come over and offer the prayers of their tradition, I could not fathom someone in my house wearing a shirt with that slogan. I decided that I had to act. By asking Omar to change his shirt, I was standing up for myself, in support of my tradition and my home.

On the back of the T-shirt from Face to Face, there is a quote by historian Howard Zinn: "We don't have to engage in grand, heroic actions to participate in the process of change. Small acts, when multiplied by millions of people, can transform the world." I agree with Zinn. However, how one decides to do this can be ethically complex. This experience at Face to Face has caused me to reflect upon how difficult it is to make the "right" decision in every situation. Finding a common meeting point is a necessary first step, but it is not sufficient by itself. The challenge in following through after that first step is actually listening to what the other person is saying. I know I will encounter many more such challenging situations in my life. Nonetheless, I will not attempt to avoid them. Instead, I hope that I can accommodate the beliefs and opinions of those who are different from me—as I did here—while still standing up for what I believe.

PEACE

AN EYE FOR AN EYE ONLY ENDS UP MAKING
THE WHOLE WORLD BLIND.

Mahatma Gandhi

✦

THE FIRST PEACE, WHICH IS THE MOST IMPORTANT,
IS THAT WHICH COMES FROM WITHIN THE SOULS OF PEOPLE
WHEN THEY REALIZE THEIR RELATIONSHIP, THEIR ONENESS WITH THE
UNIVERSE AND ALL ITS POWERS, AND WHEN THEY REALIZE THAT AT THE
CENTER OF THE UNIVERSE DWELLS THE GREAT SPIRIT, AND THAT THIS
CENTER IS REALLY EVERYWHERE, IT IS WITHIN EACH OF US.

Black Elk

BLESSED ARE THE PEACEMAKERS, FOR THEY SHALL
BE CALLED THE CHILDREN OF GOD.

Jesus

✦

THE WHOLE OF THE TORAH IS FOR THE PURPOSE
OF PROMOTING PEACE.

The Talmud (Judaism)

✦

PEACE IS NOT MERELY A DISTANT GOAL THAT WE SEEK,
BUT A MEANS BY WHICH WE ARRIVE AT THAT GOAL.

Martin Luther King Jr.

✦

I CHARGE YOU ALL THAT EACH ONE OF YOU
CONCENTRATE ALL THE THOUGHTS OF YOUR HEART ON LOVE
AND UNITY. WHEN A THOUGHT OF WAR COMES, OPPOSE IT BY A
STRONGER THOUGHT OF PEACE. A THOUGHT OF HATRED MUST
BE DESTROYED BY A MORE POWERFUL THOUGHT OF LOVE. THOUGHTS
OF WAR BRING DESTRUCTION TO ALL HARMONY, WELL-BEING,
RESTFULNESS AND CONTENT. THOUGHTS OF LOVE ARE CONSTRUCTIVE
OF BROTHERHOOD, PEACE, FRIENDSHIP AND HAPPINESS.

Abdu'l-Baha (Baha'i)

✦

AND IF THEY LEAN TO PEACE, LEAN YOU ALSO TO IT,
AND PUT YOUR TRUST IN ALLAH.

The Qur'an (Islam)

THOSE WHO ARE FREE OF RESENTFUL THOUGHTS
SURELY FIND PEACE.

Buddha

✦

PEACE IS NOT THE PRODUCT OF TERROR OR FEAR.
PEACE IS NOT THE SILENCE OF CEMETERIES. PEACE IS NOT THE SILENT
RESULT OF VIOLENT REPRESSION. PEACE IS THE GENEROUS, TRANQUIL
CONTRIBUTION OF ALL TO THE GOOD OF ALL. PEACE IS DYNAMISM.
PEACE IS GENEROSITY. IT IS RIGHT AND IT IS DUTY.

Oscar Romero (Roman Catholic)

✦

IF YOU WANT PERMANENT PEACE, YOU WILL
WANT TO LEAD A DEDICATED LIFE,
CONSTANTLY LIVING FOR THE SAKE OF OTHERS.
THEN NOBODY CAN DISTURB
YOUR PEACE. THAT SACRIFICE IS THE KEY TO PEACE,
AND WITHOUT PEACE
THERE IS NO JOY OR HAPPINESS.

Sri Swami Satchidananda

CONVERSION

What will God think if I convert?

Dear Pastor Paul,

I was born and raised Jewish. I was Bat Mitzvahed, went to Hebrew school, but went to synagogue only when we "had to." Now that I'm seventeen I realize that I don't agree with a lot of Jewish teachings, and I'm in search of my own personal spirituality. My father is half Catholic, and I feel strongly that I belong in that church. I believe in my heart that it doesn't matter what your religion is as long as you love and respect God, but I also worry that I would be denying my Jewish ancestors. I am concerned that I might lose God's favor. Is there an age of consent for conversion? How would I go about doing it?

Dear Friend,

You mention that you are worried that you might lose God's favor by converting. Isn't it God who is leading you in your conversion? The first step to any conversion is a profound call through prayer and study. If your switch to Catholicism is happening because of a hunch based on your father's heritage, rather than prayerful conversations with God, you need to spend more time on the decision you are making. (You may wish to read *Girl Meets God* by Lauren Winner, which chronicles a young woman's similar dilemma.)

In answer to your "how to" question, the Catholic Church considers anyone who is at least fourteen years old capable of making a serious choice about their religion. You can call a church directly. Or, since you have Catholic relatives, why not give them a call and have them recommend a priest or lay leader who could meet with you? Either way, be prepared to attend a class called the Rite of Christian Initiation for Adults to learn about the church and its teachings. This class can take up to a year and will give you a chance to really dive into the culture of the Catholic Church and find out if it is right for you.

INTERFAITH FOCUS:

INTERFAITH YOUTH CORE

The Story of the Interfaith Youth Core, by Ebrahim Patel

MY BEST FRIENDS IN HIGH SCHOOL included a Jew, a Mormon, a Hindu and a Catholic. We were all religious to a degree, but we almost never talked about our religion with each other. We knew that certain people did not eat during particular times of the year and others were restricted from various activities on specific days, and religion played a role in these matters. But we rarely discussed these things openly. In retrospect, not only did that limit my understanding of something deep and important in my friends' lives, it pointed to a weak understanding of something deep and important in my own life. I did not know how to make my religion relevant outside of my own Muslim community.

In college, I encountered the vision of Dorothy Day and the Catholic Worker movement. Dorothy's philosophy was that Catholics should put their faith into action by providing comfort to poor people and working toward a social order where all people live in dignity. My Muslim faith called me to do the same. I spent many hours serving food to poor people at Catholic Worker Houses all over the United States. I was a Muslim working with Catholics in the common language of service. I listened to them tell stories about how Catholicism inspired them to do service, and I shared how Islam did the same for me.

I wish my high school friends and I had had that opportunity. It would have strengthened each of our connections to our own religions, helped us learn more about one another's faith and allowed us to put the service ideals of our faiths into action together. I felt so strongly about this that I decided to start an organization that would give other young people—high school and college students and beyond—that opportunity.

The name of my organization is the Interfaith Youth Core (IFYC). I founded it in 1998. The organization is based in Chicago, and our mission is to build a national interfaith youth service movement. The basic message of this movement is simple: If you are young and religious in America, you should be coming together with other young religious people to serve society.

In addition to helping people, you will strengthen your own faith identity and build understanding with people from different religions. You will also be taking an important step toward world peace by being a living example that people of different religions can work together in positive ways.

(See Appendix pages 230–31 for the Interfaith Youth Core's Code of Conduct.)

How can I get started on being Buddhist?

Dear Pastor Paul,

I stopped worshiping God after my grandfather's death a few months ago and want to become Buddhist. The problem is, I don't know where to start. My family, who raised me as a Catholic and remain very religious Catholics, does not know I've stopped worshiping God or that I want to change my religion. It's going to be very hard to tell them, especially my grandma. (She became very angry with me when I stopped eating meat recently.) So I have two questions: How do I tell my family, and how do I get started on being Buddhist?

Dear Friend,

Before I answer your questions, answer this one: Is your changing of religions a reaction to your grandfather's death and some subconscious desire to punish God? If so, you may wish to reflect more on your decision. We all will experience the death of loved ones, and we also must come to grips with our own death. Your grandfather's death, by itself, is not a valid reason for your desire to start your Buddhist practice.

On the other hand, if the way Buddhism addresses the reality of death rings true to you, and you want to dedicate your life to that path, then Buddhism may be the religion for you.

As long as you are living in your parents' house, you should continue to honor your parents' religion and go to church with them. Compassion is an important part of Buddhism, and obviously it means a lot to your parents that you take part in their religion. While you are fulfilling your duties to your family, you may want to continue your study of Buddhism by reading books by the Dalai Lama and others. Once you are on your own, it is very important that you find a Buddhist community, or *sangha*, that will help you along your way.

CELEBRITY SPIRITUALITY

Q: What attracts you to Buddhism?

"The feeling I get from the rinpoches [spiritual leaders] and his Holiness the Dalai Lama and Tibetan people in general. The people that I've met are really centered in the heart; they're coming from a real clear, compassionate place. And most of the teachings that I've read about almost seem set up to distract the other side of your brain in order to give your heart center a chance to open up. In terms of what I understand, Buddhism is like a manual to achieve enlightenment—there are these five things and these six things within the first thing, and all these little subdivisions. And despite all of that right-brain information, it's very heart centered. At least that's the feeling I get from the Tibetans. Also the teachings of Tibetan Buddhism have been passed down for a long time now. They have that system pretty well figured out."

Adam Yauch from the Beastie Boys in the interview at *www.tricycle.com*

How can I tell my parents I've converted to Islam?

Dear Pastor Paul,

I have converted to Islam. My family are Pentecostal Christians. How do I tell them? I'm going to be graduating soon, and I'm thinking of just not saying anything until after I'm out of the house.

Dear Friend,

It's tough not being able to share who you are and what you believe with your family, but I think you are right on about waiting until you're out of the house and independent before you tell them about your conversion. Not only could things get ugly, but honoring your parents is in keeping with your new faith tradition. So while you're still in your parents' house, try to follow their rules and beliefs as best you can.

Once you're on your own, explain your beliefs to your family in language they will understand. I suggest you emphasize that both Islam and Christianity (and Judaism, for that matter) worship God, but in different ways.

Ultimately, converting from your family's religion is a lonely affair. However, as long as you remain a loving daughter and sister, they'll eventually accept you and your new beliefs.

CELEBRITY SPIRITUALITY

"Allah says in the Qur'an not to despise one another. So the criterion in Islam is not color or social status. It's who is most righteous. If I go to a mosque—and I'm a basketball player with money and prestige—if I go to a mosque and see an imam, I feel inferior. He's better than me. It's about knowledge."

Hakeem Olajuwon in the *Beliefnet* interview by Deborah Caldwell

Why I'm Muslim
by Musa Syeed

There were no decorations, no camera-happy uncles. There wasn't even any food to bribe people to come. Although it was no kind of formal rite of passage, in those ten minutes that I stood at the front of the mosque, I left boyhood behind and remembered why I love my way of life.

My pubescent voice was squeakier than a rusty tricycle when I first led the prayer in my mosque. The eldest—or at least the most knowledgeable—adult normally leads, the job usually going to the parents. But for whatever reason, that day there weren't too many parents around. That day, those parents who were around pushed me to the front to lead everyone.

Responsibility, a word teenagers cringe at, was heaped upon me thirty times over. My followers charged me with the duty of guiding them from beginning to end of the prayer, leading them through all the standing, bowing and kneeling, without screwing up. And since Islam is a religion for the people, the prayer had to fit everyone's needs. I had to be mindful of the small children's short attention spans, of the mothers whose minds were on their small children, and of the old men whose bones crackled each time they knelt to the floor. I had to exhibit one of the most valued qualities in Islam—mercy. Holding the responsibility of thirty

- People who practice the religion called Islam are Muslims.

- Branches of Islam: Sunni, Shiite.

- Muslims worship in a mosque or masjid.

- An Islamic religious leader is an imam.

- Age: 1,500 years

- Country of origin: Saudi Arabia

- Number of American Muslims: 4 million

- Number of Muslims worldwide: 1.3 billion

- Time in USA: 300+ years

people in your hands for just ten minutes can be an exasperating experience.

And with all that mounting responsibility, my connection to God grew deeper. I thanked God for allowing me to be trusted with that type of responsibility. I thanked God for being so loving of young people, for saving a special place in the shade of his throne for those who spend their youth righteously. I thanked God for this gift of guidance.

I love being a Muslim because Islam is about empowering the individual to spread goodness, whether that be leading a prayer or finding the cure for cancer. After those ten minutes, being a teenager only meant I belonged to a certain age group, not ruled by a certain state of mind. There was no reason for me to get into teenage rebellion because Islam empowered me. I realized that adolescence might have made me taller, but Islam made me a man.

How can I convert to Judaism?

Dear Pastor Paul,

Hi, I am fifteen years old and have been studying Judaism for three years. I have decided I want to convert. I have told my dad, who I live with, and he supports and accepts my beliefs. I am not sure what to do now. Should I contact a rabbi, go to synagogue, and/or Torah study? If you could answer my questions that would be a lot of help. Thank you.

Dear Friend,

Each Jewish denomination (Reform, Conservative and Orthodox) has different requirements for people who wish to convert. You should first visit synagogues from several of the different denominational backgrounds to see which one appeals to you on the deepest level. Once you have found a community that you would like to join, contact the rabbi. Just be aware that the act of converting to Judaism, like any other conversion, takes time and a real commitment. However, it sounds like you have been diligent in your studies and are ready to take such a big step.

How do I leave my church?

Dear Pastor Paul,

I am planning on leaving my church because I am no longer growing spiritually in that place, but I don't want to offend my youth pastor or the head pastor . . . what should I do??

Dear Friend,

Your question shows a lot of compassion, and that will help you to make this transition. I suggest you first meet with your youth pastor to tell him or her how you're feeling. It could be that they only need more guidance in how to help you with your religious development for you to want to stay. But if you're convinced you want to go, don't feel guilty! Write a letter thanking your pastor and youth pastor for all they've done for you. Tell them you want to experience other communities, giving your reasons honestly and uncritically. They should understand: A gauge of a good pastor is how well they let go.

Why I'm a Member of the Church of Jesus Christ of Latter-Day Saints (Mormon)

by Francisco R. Nava

My conversion to the Church of Jesus Christ of Latter-Day Saints rests on an empowering line of scripture in the Epistle of James: "If any of you lack wisdom, let him ask of God, that giveth to all men liberally, and upbraideth not; and it shall be given him." The wisdom I lacked at the age of eighteen concerned whether or not the Book of Mormon, the keystone of the Mormon faith, was true and whether the church's founder, Joseph Smith, was a prophet of God. So much was hingeing on my decision. I had been a very devout and confirmed Roman Catholic; my family was very religious and would most certainly be offended if I left the religion of my upbringing and of my ancestors. To be Mormon would mean a change in my lifestyle: I would dress modestly; I would forever abstain from alcohol and coffee; I would refrain from using profanities; I would pay a full tithe, giving one-tenth of my income to the church; I would attend services that last three times longer than the one-hour Catholic Mass I attended on Sundays; and I would most of all be responsible for sharing my newfound faith with others. I sorely needed wisdom, for I was at a veritable crossroads in my life.

However anxious I felt about what my family would say, or about seeing myself in a different religion, I found the words of James to be quite comforting. His directive was simple: Pray to God for wisdom. Prayer is a gift that belongs to everyone—Catholics and Mormons alike. So, once having read the Book of Mormon, I sequestered myself in my room for several hours and kneeled down to pray with the counsel of James in my thoughts. There at my bedside I communed with the Almighty in a way that I could feel his affirming utterances throughout my body. God had opened his divinity unto me and answered what I needed to know. The Book of Mormon had brought me to my knees in my first conference with God, and it continues to inspire such conversations again and again.

Now I am a Mormon young man. My family still loves me and respects my faith. They all agree that my words are cleaner, that my disposition is calmer and that my love for God is greater. I am now preparing to serve a two-year mission for my church and to invite others to pray, as I do, for God's wisdom.

CHAPTER 11

SHARING YOUR RELIGION

Why won't people understand my Buddhist friend?

Dear Pastor Paul,

My friend recently started practicing Buddhism. Her aunt and uncle nearly flipped when she tried to explain that she didn't believe in God, didn't want eternal life in Paradise, and that Hitler wasn't an evil man but a man with evil intentions. Her sister couldn't understand why she wasn't crying her eyes out when her parents divorced.

I'm pretty comfortable with her new religion, as are the rest of our friends, but I feel sorry for her. She's tried to educate people about her religion, but nobody seems to listen. They believe Buddhism is the work of the devil and that the Buddha is a false idol. Is there anything I can do for her? Is there anything she can do to not be singled out?

Dear Friend,

It's very difficult to begin to practice a different religion in a hostile environment, especially your own home. One way your friend can avoid being singled out is to practice her Buddhism less by instructing people on the tenets of her new religion than by exhibiting one of the most important practices of Buddhism: compassion.

Your friend shouldn't feel surprised when people react strongly to her professions of her Buddhist beliefs. In the aunt and uncle's religion, she is risking hell by saying she doesn't believe in God. This belief is as real for them as your friend's Buddhist beliefs are for her. Also, the middle of her parents' divorce might not be the right time to talk with her distraught sister about the Buddhist principle of nonattachment. Being a comfort to her sister's pain, even if she doesn't feel it, is the best way she can educate people about Buddhism and its positive effect on people's lives.

You are already doing your part by treating her the same way you always have. If she is not already a member of a Buddhist practice center, she should join one to gain additional support and instruction.

Why I'm Buddhist

by Dana Graef

The *zendo*, or meditation hall, is filled with people blasting madly into their noisemakers. All of the lights in the Zen Center are turned on and every door is open. Fresh flowers are placed throughout the impeccably cleaned house. For sixty furious, reverberating seconds, the monitor stands at the top of the hall with his arm raised while everyone is tooting into horns, shaking rattles together, banging pots and pans, and clacking spoons. Midnight, and his arm drops the room into silence. "Happy New Year!" we call out to one another. "May peace prevail on Earth!"

We are seated to take the Buddhist precepts, guidelines to follow in life. Hands palm to palm, we repeat: "I resolve not to kill, but to cherish all life. . . ."

We file out of the *zendo*, collect white candles, and return for the reading of the New Year's Prayer. I stand silently in the circle, mesmerized by my candle's flame, the gathering hot wax, and the limitless, all-encompassing prayer:

"May those who are starving be given food. . . . May the sick be healed. . . . May wars and violence be no more. . . . May everyone be whole and filled with compassion. . . . At this moment, the beginning of a New Year, we earnestly beseech that peace shall come into the hearts of all people, that strife and dissension shall be no more."

JUST THE FAQS BUDDHISM

- A person who follows the teachings of the Buddha is a Buddhist.

- Major Branches: Theravada, Mahayana, Tibetan

- Buddhists practice their religion in temples, dharma centers and shrines.

- A Buddhist leader is called a priest, monk, nun, lama.

- A few of the primary sacred writings are Dhammapada; Pali Canon (Tripitaka); The Sutras (including the Lotus Sutra, the Diamond Sutra, the Heart Sutra and others).

- Age: 2,500 years

- Country of origin: Nepal and India

- Number of American Buddhists: More than 1 million

- Number of Buddhists worldwide: 360 million

- Time in USA: 130 years (beginning with the first Japanese immigrants to the U.S. in the 1870s)

The ceremony concludes with the ringing of temple bells, and we gather for eggnog, cakes and hot cocoa. After having cleansed our houses and minds, eliminating the detritus that has collected over the past year, the Buddhist community has celebrated the beginning of a new year.

Ever since I was old enough to stay awake until midnight, I have spent December 31 at the Zen Center with my family. Indeed, Buddhism has been synonymous with my life for the past twenty years. It is not something that I like or dislike any more than I would like or dislike my own existence. It simply is. I have always been thankful that I was raised within a religion that, paradoxically, does not impose rules. Instead, the Buddha warned his students against blindly accepting any teachings, even his own. I was raised in an unusual manner in America, by parents who never imposed their own desires on what their children ultimately decided to do. Because no one has attempted to answer every question that I have posed, I have learned to wonder. Who am I? Where am I going? Why am I here? These questions are the very essence of Buddhist practice—the questions themselves. No one else can tell you precisely who and what you are; so where would you begin to look for the answers?

Buddhism is a constant search for the unknown. Following a Buddhist lifestyle, I have learned from my parents' example: Don't tell other people what is best for them. Allow them to make their own mistakes, because they won't learn anything that is forced upon them. Listen with complete attention. Not everything needs to be revealed at once. Never place limits on anyone's potential. Every moment of every day is as precious as the next; there is no one holy day. Buddhism is a challenge to respect all beings, to live in the here and now. It is belief in what we may not see—that peace prevails on Earth.

Why are my friends
resisting my religion?

Dear Pastor Paul,

Last year I was saved and I am now a disciple of the Lord. Jesus Christ has been such a wonderful blessing in my life, and I want to share the gift of salvation that God has given me with my friends. I have tried to witness to them, but they have not always responded the way I would like. My friend told me to stop talking about God with her or she wouldn't hang around me anymore. This hurts so much. I feel as if she's trying to make me choose between my faith and her. What should I do?

Dear Friend,

You are in the tough position many people find themselves in after a religious transformation. Your beliefs are so strong and your new life has been so wonderful, you want everyone to know the joy you feel. Your friends should understand that this is very important to you, listen to you and be happy for you. However, you cannot force them to have the same experience as you have had. Their lives are unique, and their experience will continue to be unique to them.

Instead of trying to tell them what to believe, why don't you start by having a conversation about what you all believe about God in a less confrontational way? Perhaps you could all bring or make a piece of art or music that is a representation of your experience of God, or go to a museum to look at the way people's experience of God has been depicted throughout the ages. In the end, these discussions will deepen your friendships and may even allow your belief—and your friends' beliefs—to deepen.

Art

Art, like music, has always been used to convey spiritual feeling and belief. Think Sistine Chapel or statues of Buddha.

Religious art is an interpretation of spiritual truths from the artist's perspective. Making art can be also be a spiritual practice for you. Creativity is in itself a spiritual exercise in which you offer your unique gifts and insights to the world. "The primary benefit of practicing any art, whether well or badly," wrote novelist Kurt Vonnegut Jr., "is that it enables one's soul to grow."

Spiritual Activity #1
Create with spirit.

Decide upon a spiritual theme for an art exhibit with your friends. Give each person a camera and two hours to take photographs on a spiritual theme such as God, ecstasy or peace. The same thing can be done with paints or collages from magazines. Give the artists the opportunity to explain the spiritual elements in their work.

Spiritual Activity #2
Learn from the masters.

When you visit art galleries, keep an eye out for the photo, painting or sculpture that affects you most deeply. Stand a while and figure out what it is that touches you about the artwork. Some of the most inspiring art can be done by people just like you who are using their creativity to explore the deep questions with which they are wrestling. While some of these artists may have unorthodox ideas, it will always be thought provoking. Go with some friends to talk about what you saw and how you each interpreted the artistic expression.

Why does my friend tell me I killed Jesus?

Dear Pastor Paul,

Because I'm Jewish, a friend of mine thinks it is funny to tell me I killed Jesus. First he says it as a joke, but he is serious. He resents me as a Jewish man because of it, which I find ridiculous. Second, I understand Jesus was killed by the Romans. Please answer this question for me. Who killed Jesus?

Dear Friend,

Jesus was a Jewish man. So saying Jews killed Jesus is like saying Americans killed Abraham Lincoln because John Wilkes Booth was American. As a political matter the crucifixion was the result of Jesus' conflict with his own religious leaders, who acted in collusion with the Roman occupying force to have him killed. In theological terms, Christians believe that all played a part in Jesus' death. Because of humanity's sinful nature, Jesus underwent death and resurrection to conquer sin and death, offering salvation to the world.

Your "friend" is parroting a political position that has been used as a rationale for an incredible amount of bloodshed and oppression against the Jews over the last two thousand years.

Tell your friend that it's not only false, but that it hurts your feelings.

INTERFAITH FOCUS:

INTERFAITH MINISTRIES

INTERFAITH MINISTRIES FOR Greater Houston's Youth Leadership Council is a place where diversity is celebrated, community is served and ideas are nurtured. The Youth Leadership Council is a dynamic panel of high school leaders who come together to discuss topical issues of faith, travel to various houses of worship, and plan exciting and fun interfaith activities. Reaching beyond tolerance to respect is the goal of this group, whose members will be the ones who will truly change the world.

In the nonthreatening environment of the panel's monthly meetings, members learn leadership and diplomacy skills to work with peers of varied cultural and faith backgrounds; communication skills to convey information about themselves and their faith; critical thinking skills to process information and apply lessons; and a sense of civic-mindedness that recognizes the importance of public service.

During one meeting the Council asked themselves what they had learned from being on the Youth Leadership Council with young people of different faiths. Here were some of their responses:

- I used to think Hindus worship cows, but I've come to respect the many symbols and rituals of their faith.
- I used to think that to learn about other faiths was being untrue to my own, but I've learned to worship mine, but respect all.
- I used to think the Jain nuns covered their mouths when they spoke because of fear of germs, but I've learned that their concept of practicing nonviolence even extends to the microorganisms in the air reacting to their warm breath, along with the remembrance that we must think before we speak so as to not wound another with unkind words.
- I used to view Jewish practices as rigid or weird, but now I've learned that these traditions are followed to remind Jews of God's promises and his faithfulness to them in the past.
- I used to think I was well-informed about world religions, but I've learned that book knowledge about a particular faith doesn't compare to having real relationships with someone from another faith.

- I used to think my faith was the only one that had felt discrimination, but I learned through the personal sharing of my Muslim friends what they've had to deal with since September 11.
- I used to believe that if my faith is right, then one that believed differently was wrong, but I've come to believe that there are many paths to God.

Is there any such thing as coincidence?

Dear Pastor Paul,

I'm thirteen and Methodist. My question is, Is there such a thing as coincidence? I believe coincidences are all God's doing, but my friend doesn't buy it. In every example from our lives my friend mentions, I see more clearly that God is working all the time, and I've come to believe that it's not coincidence. I've tried to convince her so many times that I get a little mad at her.

I argued with her night after night online. Then I don't know what happened. We talked about all religious stuff, and she doesn't even seem to want to be my friend that much anymore because ever since I got confirmed I have been a lot more into God.

Dear Friend,

Badgering your friend will not make your friend believe in God. Even if it did, her faith would be very shallow, and she would abandon it at the first sign of trouble.

Very rarely do people come to faith in God through argument or attempts at proof, which is what you are offering your friend. People usually come to faith through their family's tradition, or through personal experience or testimony.

Only when she sees her life as part of a much larger truth will your friend be open to knowing God. For someone who counts her life as part of a cosmic whole, there is no differentiating between God and coincidence, as all things flow from the same source.

If it's not too late, I suggest you invite your friend to a non-confrontational prayer or meditation group. Or simply offer your own testimony of God, and remain a loving presence in her life. In the end your example will be much more convincing than anger or argument.

Can I help God by being famous?

Dear Pastor Paul,

I am totally obsessed with being famous. My friend from youth group says that God doesn't want us to be famous, just to do the best we can for others. But I feel like my being famous would help the world to know about God and that God would appreciate that. Which one of us is right?

Dear Friend,

What would you do to make yourself famous? Famous people are not always admirable, and some do very bad things in their drive to be famous. God doesn't need famous people. God needs good people to let the world know about God by living generous, joyful and exemplary lives that reflect God's goodness. Why not just concentrate on being a decent and loving person, and if you wind up being famous for it, that's great!

CELEBRITY SPIRITUALITY

Q: Why do you call your show The Divine Performance?
"We look at the spiritual life as a performance before God. God is the headliner, and the stage is the world, and so you're always an opening act, no matter how popular and successful you become. So you never really perform in a complete sense, like I did and ended my performance. What you're doing is opening for God."

KRS-One in the *Beliefnet* interview by Mark LeVine

CELEBRITY SPIRITUALITY

Circle or write down the letter in front of the response that most closely corresponds to your belief.

1. In the song by Pink, what is God?
- A. One of us
- B. The Big Lover
- C. A DJ

2. Which Final Fantasy creature does NOT take its name from a religious being?
- A. Ifrit (Muslim demon)
- B. Xena (Zoroastrian angel)
- C. Shiva (Hindu god)

3. The Taoist idea that a life force flows through all things appears in what movie series?
- A. The *Matrix* trilogy
- B. The *Terminator* movies
- C. The *Star Wars* saga

4. In his album *Play*, Moby made remixes of this form of African American religious expression.
- A. Soul
- B. Spiritual
- C. Reggae

5. How is the teenage star of TV's *Joan of Arcadia* like the French Catholic saint Joan of Arc?
- A. She conquers Anglo-Saxons
- B. She prays for five hours every day
- C. God speaks to her and gives her specific instructions

6. The lead character in *Dharma & Greg* is named after:
- A. A type of Buddhist ancestor worship
- B. The Sanskrit word for teachings, used in both Buddhism and Hinduism
- C. A gray-green river in India

7. Video games like Resident Evil and Silent Hill feature zombies, a concept that movies have sensationalized but that originally stemmed from:
- A. Saharan Yoruba
- B. Haitian vodun
- C. Parsi rituals

8. With their focus on the Bible and witnessing to others, the Simpsons' Ned Flanders and his family are:
- A. Messianic Jews
- B. Mainline Christians
- C. Evangelical Christians

9. In *Terminator II*, a teenage John Connor tells Arnold Schwarzenegger what he can't do to humans. Which of the Ten Commandments is Connor reinforcing?
- A. Thou shalt not steal
- B. Thou shalt not kill
- C. Thou shalt not covet

10. In some versions of Final Fantasy, the focus on nature spirits, energy and elemental forces is reminiscent of what Japanese religion?

A. Shinto
B. Methodism
C. Yoga

11. In the movie *Groundhog Day*, Bill Murray has to relive a day until he gets it right. What Hindu concept of life cycles is similar?

A. Reincarnation
B. Day of Brahma
C. Hatha yoga

12. The video game Hitman was criticized for having the player kill men in orange turbans. In what religion do men typically wear turbans?

A. Islam
B. Hinduism
C. Sikhism

13. In the *Harry Potter* series, Severus Snape has renounced his allegiance to the evil Voldemort and is trying to help Dumbledore. This is an example of what religious concept?

A. Confirmation
B. Proselytization
C. Redemption

14. Pop singer Madonna is interested in Jewish mysticism, also known as:

A. Mitzvah
B. Kabbalah
C. Hashanah

15. In the song "I Still Haven't Found What I'm Looking For," U2's Bono sings "I believe in the Kingdom Come." What prayer is alluded to here?

A. The Guardian Angel Prayer
B. The Lord's Prayer/Our Father
C. The Sh'ma

16. The Simpsons' Apu has a shrine to this elephant-headed Hindu god, the remover of obstacles:

A. Ganesh
B. Vishnu
C. Isis

17. In the *Matrix*, the last human holdout is named after the promised land/heavenly Jerusalem of the Bible called:

A. Corinth
B. Zion
C. Bathsheba

18. The Wu Tang Clan, Public Enemy and Busta Rhymes have referred to what African American religious group in their lyrics?

A. The Black Panthers
B. Baha'is
C. Nation of Islam

19. When she planned to marry Ben Affleck, J. Lo had received an annulment from a previous marriage. An annulment is:

A. A Muslim decree of divorce initiated by the wife
B. A Catholic decree that a marriage was not sacramentally valid
C. A Presbyterian divorce proceeding

20. Chuppahs have appeared in both *Will and Grace* and *Gilmore Girls*. What is a chuppah?

A. A bouquet used in Christian weddings
B. A canopy used in Jewish weddings
C. A ribbon used in Hindu weddings

21. What object in *The Lord of the Rings* symbolizes the corrupting power of greed?

A. Golem's book
B. The ring
C. The elf's bow and arrow

22. Which rapper's second album refers to John 3:36: "He who believes in the Son has eternal life; he who does not obey the Son shall not see life, but the wrath of God rests upon him"?

A. Eminem
B. Outkast
C. Ja Rule

23. Which recording artist did NOT undergo a religious conversion and become more involved in Christianity?

A. Mary J. Blige
B. P. Diddy Combs
C. Snoop Dogg

24. What star of *Eight Crazy Nights* sang "Put on your yarmulke, here comes Hanukkah" on *Saturday Night Live*?

A. Adam Sandler
B. Steve Martin
C. Ralph Mateo

25. Which Destiny's Child singer/solo artist says she can be "bootylicious" and religious at the same time?

A. Eve
B. Beyoncé
C. Kelly Land

26. Which band is NOT associated with Christianity?

A. POD
B. Creed
C. Nickelback

27. Norah Jones is the daughter of which famous Hindu musician?

A. Amitabh Ghosh
B. Ravi Shankar
C. George Harrison

28. In the *X-Men* series, the character Nightcrawler spent time in a:

A. Catholic monastery
B. Jewish rabbinical training program
C. Protestant seminary

29. In which video game do you get to play God by creating and guiding a civilization?

A. Black & White
B. Grand Theft Auto
C. Halo

30. Celebrity Matchup

Tom Cruise	Buddhist
Michael Jackson	Catholic
Richard Gere	Scientology
Jennifer Lopez	Muslim
Mos Def	Jehovah's Witness
Britney Spears	Baptist

BONUS ROUND:
Match the *Simpsons* character to a religion

Lisa	Hindu
Apu	Buddhist
Ned Flanders	Jewish
Krusty the Clown	Evangelical Christian

Krusty the Clown/Jewish
Ned Flanders/Evangelical Christian
Apu/Hindu
Lisa/Buddhist
Britney Spears/Baptist
Richard Gere/Buddhist
Jennifer Lopez/Catholic
Mos Def/Muslim
Tom Cruise/Scientology
Michael Jackson/Jehovah's Witness

1. C   3. C   5. C   7. B   9. B   11. A   13. C   15. B   17. B   19. B   21. B   23. C   25. B   27. B   29. A
2. B   4. B   6. B   8. C   10. A   12. C   14. B   16. A   18. C   20. B   22. C   24. A   26. C   28. A

Will other religious people go to hell?

Dear Pastor Paul,

I only started to believe in God this summer, after I read some of the *Left Behind* series. It struck me hard, and now I'm questioning a lot of things. How do we know which religion is right? I'm Catholic, but I have a friend who is Hindu. Is she going to go to heaven when she dies? Or is she condemned to hell because she isn't Christian?

Dear Friend,

As you can probably tell, I don't believe everyone has to be a Christian to go to heaven and be loved by God. Jesus loved people who followed religions different from his own, such as the Samaritans (John 4), the Canaanite (Matthew 15) and the Centurion (Luke 7). All these people were outside of the Jewish tradition, yet Jesus associated with them and loved them, even though Jewish law did not permit it.

I stick with my core belief that God is love and that anything that is of love is of God. That's a good test for your friends of different faiths: Does their religion promote love? Hinduism believes in a supreme God and calls upon all people to revere and love all forms of life. For me, this passes the test.

LOVE

FOR ONE HUMAN BEING TO LOVE ANOTHER:
THAT IS PERHAPS THE MOST DIFFICULT OF OUR TASKS, THE ULTIMATE,
THE LAST TEST AND PROOF, THE WORK FOR WHICH
ALL OTHER WORK IS BUT PREPARATION.

Rainer Maria Rilke

✦

IF I SPEAK IN THE TONGUES OF MEN AND OF ANGELS,
BUT HAVE NOT LOVE, I AM ONLY A RESOUNDING GONG OR A
CLANGING CYMBAL. IF I HAVE THE GIFT OF PROPHECY AND
CAN FATHOM ALL MYSTERIES AND ALL KNOWLEDGE,
AND IF I HAVE A FAITH THAT CAN MOVE MOUNTAINS, BUT HAVE
NOT LOVE, I AM NOTHING. IF I GIVE ALL I POSSESS TO THE POOR
AND SURRENDER MY BODY TO THE FLAMES, BUT HAVE NOT LOVE
I GAIN NOTHING. LOVE IS PATIENT, LOVE IS KIND. IT DOES NOT ENVY,
IT DOES NOT BOAST, IT IS NOT PROUD. IT IS NOT RUDE,
IT IS NOT SELF-SEEKING, IT IS NOT EASILY ANGERED, IT KEEPS NO
RECORD OF WRONGS. LOVE DOES NOT DELIGHT IN EVIL BUT
REJOICES WITH THE TRUTH. IT ALWAYS PROTECTS, ALWAYS TRUSTS,
ALWAYS PERSEVERES. LOVE NEVER FAILS. BUT WHERE THERE
ARE PROPHECIES, THEY WILL CEASE; WHERE THERE ARE TONGUES, THEY
WILL BE STILLED; WHERE THERE IS KNOWLEDGE, IT WILL PASS AWAY. . . .
AND NOW THESE THINGS REMAIN: FAITH, HOPE AND LOVE.
BUT THE GREATEST OF THESE IS LOVE.

1 Corinthians 13:1–8, 13

YOUR TASK IS NOT TO SEEK FOR LOVE,
BUT MERELY TO SEEK AND FIND ALL THE BARRIERS WITHIN
YOURSELF THAT YOU HAVE BUILT AGAINST IT.

Rumi

✦

THE MOMENT YOU HAVE IN YOUR HEART
THIS EXTRAORDINARY THING CALLED LOVE AND FEEL THE DEPTH,
THE DELIGHT, THE ECSTASY OF IT, YOU WILL DISCOVER
THAT FOR YOU THE WORLD IS TRANSFORMED.

J. Krishnamurti

✦

LOVE YOUR NEIGHBOR AS YOURSELF.

Jesus

✦

TO LOVE SOMEONE DEEPLY GIVES YOU STRENGTH.
BEING LOVED BY SOMEONE DEEPLY
GIVES YOU COURAGE.

Lao-tzu

✦

WHERE LOVE IS—NO ROOM IS TOO SMALL.

The Talmud

WE CAN DO NO GREAT THINGS;
ONLY SMALL THINGS WITH GREAT LOVE.

Mother Teresa

◆

ONE WORD FREES US OF ALL THE WEIGHT AND PAIN OF LIFE:
THAT WORD IS LOVE.

Sophocles

CHAPTER 12

RELIGIONS 101

BUDDHISM

If you visit:

Helpful terms

Bodhisattva—a spiritual being who is well advanced toward enlightenment and helps others advance toward enlightenment

Gassho—placing palms together in reverence

Karma—the understanding that each action has a consequence that can be manifested in this life or in the next life

Koan—a question that cannot be answered with the intellect, prompting deeper spiritual inquiry; a riddle or a tale used to teach a Buddhist principle

Mandala—a geometric design that focuses meditation

Mantra—a sound, word or phrase said in repetition in meditation or for another religious purpose

Mudras—hand gestures that convey various meanings within Buddhism

Samatha—stopping and calming through meditation

Stupa—a burial ground or shrine that is said to contain a relic of the Buddha or important Buddhists

Vipassana—looking deeply through meditation, leading to insight

Zazen—"sitting" meditation that consists of clearing of the mind

Where should I go?

Many different traditions of Buddhism are practiced in America. Which kind of center you should attend will depend on what kind of experience you are looking for. Many Asian temples' style and form of Buddhism correspond to the culture of a specific country and may be conducted in that country's native language. Centers founded by Westerners are often less ritualistic and more meditation focused. A good way to decide is to check the Internet or the *Yellow Pages* under "Religion" or "Churches" for a Buddhist center near you. The Web site *www.Buddhanet.net*, also has an extensive, up-to-date list of centers around the world.

Once you find a center, call ahead to see when meditation classes or services are held and if visitors are welcome. In general, you will find Buddhist groups visitor-friendly, and you should not be afraid to attend an introductory workshop or a formal service.

What should I wear?

Whenever you go to any new religious or spiritual group you should look presentable. In a Buddhist setting it's a good idea to wear comfortable and modest clothing (no tight jeans or skirts) as much of the time is spent sitting in meditation. As a rule you may wish to dress a bit nicer for Asian-American temples. Wear clothes that are flexible enough to allow for sitting on a mat on the floor, or on a chair. Some meditation halls can be very large and drafty while others can be too hot, so wear some layers. You may wish to wear dark or muted clothing as bright colors are considered distracting to others.

Should I bring money?

Bring a little money with you in order to make a small donation, either up front at the altar or in a basket that will be marked.

What will I see?

You will likely see a statue of the Buddha within the shrine and observe practitioners bowing to the Buddha. This is a sign of respect for the teachings of the Buddha as well as an acknowledgment of each person's own true nature. The walls may have depictions of Bodhisattvas, which are spiritual beings that help others to attain enlightenment. You may also encounter a *stupa*, which is a dome-like sacred structure containing a relic. Devotees sometimes walk around the dome in a clockwise direction, carrying flowers and incense as a sign of reverence. Some *stupas* can be as big as temples themselves.

What should I do?

Some temple services will resemble a church, with a bulletin, chairs to sit in and even a chanting book. Other centers will be more sparse with mats on the floor, less ritual activity and more meditation. Some centers have a place near the entrance where you can leave your shoes, but not all Buddhist centers do this so be observant and do what others do. Feel free to ask a greeter about the custom of the service if it isn't clear to you. Let the other people present be your guide—if someone bows to you, bow back; if someone extends their hand, shake it. Be respectful of nuns and monks. Do not initiate physical contact with them as handshaking may not be allowed for them.

Make sure you have time to stay for the entire service or meditation as it is considered very bad behavior to leave in the middle of a formal meditation. *Turn off your cell phone!*

Adherents of different Buddhist traditions and Buddhists from different countries and cultures celebrate different holidays.

Rohatsu—December

In Japanese, Rohatsu literally means the eighth day of the twelfth lunar month. It is a Zen Buddhist holiday commemorating the anniversary of the Buddha's enlightenment under the Bodhi tree. It is a time for practitioners to rededicate themselves to their practice with intense meditation for a week, beginning on December 1 and lasting through December 8.

Losar—February

Losar is the Tibetan New Year and is held at the time of the winter solstice. This is the most important holiday in Tibet. Celebrations include cleansing and purification rituals to get rid of bad influences from the past year, as well as a lot of feasting and fun.

Vesak—Buddha's Birthday

A celebration of the birth of the Buddha. It is the most important holiday for Theravadan Buddhists.

Basic tenets

The Three Jewels

The essential components of Buddhism are the Three Jewels (or the Three Refuges): the Buddha, the Dharma (his teachings) and the Sangha (the followers of those teachings). An expression of intention for many Buddhists is "I take refuge in the Buddha, I take refuge in the Dhamma, and I take refuge in the Sangha." Taking refuge means following the path from suffering to liberation—the path to ultimate freedom.

The First Jewel: The Buddha

Siddhartha Gautama was born a prince in the sixth century BCE in a kingdom known as Kapilavastu, located in present-day Nepal. Before he was born, sages predicted he would become either a spiritual leader or a king. Spiritual leadership was not what Siddhartha's father had in mind for his son, who he expected would follow him as ruler of the province. To prevent Siddhartha from leaving his palace, the king sheltered him from the harshness of life and showered luxury on him. Siddhartha eventually married a lovely princess and settled down to what his father hoped would be his intended princely life.

However, the prince ventured out one day and saw three things he had never seen before: an old person, a sick person and a corpse surrounded by mourners. He realized that his luxury, health and fine things were eventually going to change, and that all material happiness was impermanent. He was so struck by what he saw that he resolved to find the root of this suffering. Following the example of a wandering holy man, Siddhartha cut off his hair and gave up his possessions. He spent the next six years practicing the religion of the region (an early form of Hinduism). Following the practice of the ascetic, he denied himself all physical comforts, to the point of dangerously weakening his body. Ultimately he realized that extreme bodily suffering was as distracting to spiritual growth as his former indulgent luxury and decided to follow a "middle way," or a balanced approach to life.

Siddhartha sat under a tree and decided to remain there until he discovered how to liberate himself from suffering and sorrow. Under that tree, Siddhartha was able to cleanse his mind of all impurities, desires, attachments and even the "I," or the ego, which had bound him to the world. At the age of thirty-five, Siddhartha had "awakened," which is what the name Buddha means, and achieved full realization or enlightenment.

For the rest of his life the Buddha taught the Four Noble Truths—his realization of the cause of suffering—and the Eightfold Path—the solution to liberation. Together, these are the teaching of the Buddha. The original followers of the Buddha formed the first *sangha*, a community of monks and nuns. To this day a *sangha* is a community that helps individuals achieve enlightenment by teaching the Dharma, or teachings. At the age of eighty the Buddha died. His last words were, "Everything that has been created is subject to decay and death. Everything is transitory. Work out your own salvation with diligence."

The Second Jewel: The Dharma

Buddhism is a nontheistic religion, meaning there is not the same concept of God or any all-powerful, all-knowing being as understood in Christianity, Islam or Judaism. While Buddhists honor the Buddha for his wisdom in articulating the path to liberation from suffering, the Buddha is not worshiped as a deity. The Buddha rejected being proclaimed a god. When asked who he was, the Buddha simply responded, "I am awake."

There are guiding principles taught by the Buddha that all people who are striving for awakening along the Buddhist path will agree upon: the Five Moral Precepts, the Four Noble Truths and the Eightfold Path.

The Five Moral Precepts:

These five basic resolutions are the groundwork for people who wish to follow the path that the Buddha taught and lived. They are simple guidelines to living a compassionate and responsible life. People who want to follow the Five Precepts (also called the items of good character) state:

1. I resolve not to kill,
2. I resolve not to steal, but to make my livelihood in a responsible way,
3. I resolve not to misuse sexuality,
4. I resolve not to gossip, lie or slander other people, and
5. I resolve not to take drugs or cloud the mind with intoxicants, but to keep the mind clear.

The Four Noble Truths:

1. Suffering is universal and inevitable.
2. The immediate cause of suffering is craving and greed, and the ultimate cause of suffering is ignorance concerning the true nature of reality.
3. There is a way to dispel ignorance and relieve suffering by ceasing to desire and by seeing reality for what it is.
4. That way to enlightenment is to be found in the Eightfold Path.

The Eightfold Path:

1. **Right Opinion or View**—Understand the Four Noble Truths and use them as a map for life.
2. **Right Thought**—Resolve not to think impure, selfish, greedy, angry and negative thoughts.

3. **Right Speech**—Be aware that what one says matters. Avoid lying, criticizing, using harsh language or gossiping.
4. **Right Action and Conduct**—Practice the Five Precepts.
5. **Right Livelihood**—Earn money in a way that does no harm and recognize the interconnected nature of all living things.
6. **Right Effort**—Strive to practice the teachings, practice nonviolence, avoid deluded ways of thinking and maintain wholesome, positive thoughts.
7. **Right Mindfulness**—Practice self-examination and become aware of what our body and mind are feeling and thinking. Be aware and attentive at all times.
8. **Right Concentration**—Practice meditation, awareness and stability of mind.

Sacred texts

There are a great number of texts considered sacred in Buddhism. While containing the wisdom of the tradition, these texts are not considered the "word of God" but are useful for following the Buddhist path. The primary texts for Theravada Buddhism are the Pali canon, Pali being the language in which it was originally written. The Pali canon is divided into three parts called the Tripitaka or the "three baskets." The first section is called Vinaya and is dedicated to rules for the priesthood and monastic life; another section for stories and sayings of the Buddha and his disciples is called the Sutta; and a more scientific analysis of the Buddhist path is called the Abhidharma.

Mahayana scriptures include much the same material as the Theravadan texts, but in different languages. Additionally, the Buddhist texts known as the sutras have become important parts of the Mahayana canon. These include the Lotus Sutra, the Heart Sutra and the Diamond Sutra. These additional scriptures teach the uniquely Mahayana ideas such as the role and path of spiritual beings called *bodhisattvas*.

CHRISTIANITY

Helpful terms

Altar—a table in the front of the church that may have a cross on it or other sacred objects

Baptism—the Christian initiation ceremony through water

Confession—the statement of sins committed against God

Eucharist/Communion—a central Christian ritual involving bread and wine (or grape juice). It is a time of communion with Jesus Christ, with various interpretations

Icons—images of saints, Mary and Jesus common in Orthodox churches

Nave/Sanctuary—the main room of the church where services are held

Pew—benches for seating in a church

Rosary—a series of prayers and meditations related to Jesus' life and Mary's life, which Catholics say using beads

Saints—people who have lived an exemplary Christian life

Sin—an act that goes against God's will, or alienates the individual from God

Where should I go?

Going to a church you're interested in with a friend who attends regularly is always the most fun and informative. Another option is to look in your local phone book in the *Yellow Pages* under "Churches." There will be listings from various denominations. Remember, there are many different styles of worship, so the church you pick will determine the experience you have. Going to a Pentecostal church will be very different from a Greek Orthodox Church, so you may wish to try them both to see the difference. Call ahead to see about times and whether visitors are welcome. Most churches will be happy to have you. Church services are most often on Sunday mornings, but there are also some churches that worship on Saturday or Sunday night, or have

Wednesday evening services. Protestants call their worship a "service" while Catholics call it a "Mass" and Orthodox Churches call their worship time the "divine liturgy." If possible, go with a friend so you have someone to talk with about your experience.

What should I wear?

Most churches expect people to come well dressed to a Sunday service. As a visitor you are safest with a nice shirt and tie for guys and a dress or nice slacks and blouse for girls. Although some churches have a "come as you are" attitude, no one will fault you for being too dressed up. Wednesday evening services can be less formal.

Should I bring money?

Yes, some kind of donation will be expected, but you may decide the amount. Generally they will pass around a plate or basket into which you should place your donation.

What will I see?

Churches vary greatly, so what you will see depends on where you go. Many churches begin with some sort of procession towards the altar or communion table in the front of the church. The procession may consist of clergy, choir and other worship leaders. Most church services include prayers, readings from the Bible, singing, preaching and Eucharist/communion. Protestants tend to celebrate communion with less frequency than Catholics and Orthodox, although the Episcopal Church is the exception.

Catholic, Episcopal, Lutheran and Orthodox churches feature a table called an altar at the front of the church that is the focus of the service. Behind the altar is the tabernacle, a special box where the consecrated communion wafer is reverently stored, as this is considered the body of Christ. Catholic churches often have pictures, statues and stained glass depictions of the many saints recognized by the Catholic Church, as well as of Mary, the mother of Jesus, who holds a prominent place in Catholicism.

In an Orthodox church prominent features are the large, beautiful images of saints called icons that are in the front of the nave. You will also be aware of the incense that fills the room. Some Catholic, Lutheran and Episcopalian churches also use incense. If you are allergic to smoke or incense, you may have to stand away from the altar area.

In Protestant churches, preaching is very important, and you will likely see that focus is on the pulpit, an elevated area in the front of the church. A Quaker church generally has chairs arranged in a circle and there is no ritual element to the service. People will sit in silence until they feel moved by the Divine to speak.

What should I do?

In most churches you will be shown to a seat by an usher; if none are present feel free to take your own seat. Many churches have a printed order of service or a bulletin that will help you follow along. If your religious beliefs allow, it is respectful to rise when the rest of the congregation rises, kneel when others kneel and sit when others sit. You should not feel obligated to sing or speak the words of the liturgy, although you are welcome to do so. Stay in the main area of the sanctuary and do not go up to the area where the priest or minister stands, unless specifically invited. Services last anywhere from one to two or three hours in some charismatic or Orthodox churches, so you may wish to sit near the back if you think you will need to leave before the service is completed. Do your best to stay for the whole service, as it is considered impolite to leave and you should try to experience the full ceremony.

During Eucharist or communion (when Christians take the bread and wine or grape juice) visitors should politely refuse as these sacraments are only for Christians. People visiting from different Christian denominations should know that Orthodox are allowed to share in Catholic communion but Protestants are not. Neither Catholics nor Protestants are allowed to partake of the Orthodox Eucharist. Many times the minister or priest will say aloud who may partake in communion, or it may be printed in the bulletin.

In Catholic, Episcopal or Orthodox churches you may see several candles in front of an icon of Jesus, Mary or a saint. If you feel moved you should feel free to light one (sometimes a small donation is requested) and offer a prayer, perhaps for a personal issue you are wrestling with or for a loved one.

Turn off your cell phone!

Christmas

The most widely known of the Christian holidays, Christmas celebrates the birth of Jesus, Son of God in a humble manger. Many services are also held on December 24, Christmas Eve.

Epiphany (Three Kings, Tres Reyes)

This is the ending festival of the Christmas season. Since January 6 often falls on a weekday, many churches observe Epiphany on the Sunday before January 6.

Orthodox Christian Nativity of Christ

The Orthodox Christian celebration of the birth of Jesus Christ.

Ash Wednesday

Ash Wednesday is the official beginning of the forty days of Lent that culminate in Easter. It is observed with fasting and the ritual of smudging ashes in the shape of a cross on the churchgoer's forehead with the saying, "Remember you are dust, and to dust you shall return."

Palm Sunday

Commemorates the triumphal entry of Jesus into Jerusalem. Like the first-century onlookers, today's Christian may wave palms to recognize Jesus' spiritual reign.

Good Friday

Good Friday marks the day when Jesus was put on trial and put to death on the cross. Christians believe that the crucifixion of Jesus is the ultimate sacrifice that Jesus made so that all may be saved from sin. Many Christians also believe that Jesus on the cross is also a symbol of Jesus' eternal identification with those who are oppressed everywhere.

Easter Vigil

Occurs late in the evening of Holy Saturday. It is common for new converts to be baptized on this night and to celebrate the resurrection of Jesus by lighting the Christ candle or the Paschal candle. Christians remember Jesus' triumph over death by proclaiming, "Christ is risen!"

Easter

Easter Sunday officially celebrates the resurrection of Jesus and is considered the most important Christian holiday.

Pascha

The Orthodox Christian celebration of the resurrection of Jesus.

Pentecost—Catholic and Protestant (Orthodox Christian)

Commemorates the coming of the Holy Spirit to the apostles, fifty days after the resurrection of Jesus.

Basic tenets

Faith

Christianity is one of the three faiths (along with Judaism and Islam) that locate their roots in God's covenant with the patriarch Abraham. Like Islam and Judaism, Christians are monotheistic and believe in one God. However, Christians believe that God became human, or incarnate, two thousand years ago in the person of Jesus the Christ—God's son. The term "Christian" comes from the Greek word *Christos*, which means "anointed one." Christians believe that Jesus was the Messiah sent by God for the salvation of the world. Although Christianity consists of many different beliefs and practices, all Christians look toward Jesus as the central figure in their faith.

Jesus

The person known as Jesus was born into a humble Jewish family approximately two thousand years ago in the region now known as Palestine and Israel. The Christian Bible tells that the birth of Jesus was heralded by the angel Gabriel, who appeared to the Virgin Mary, Jesus' mother, saying, "Do not be afraid, Mary, for you have found favor with God. And now, you will conceive in your womb and bear a son, and you will name him Jesus. He will be great, and will be called the Son of the Most High, and the Lord God will give to him the throne of his ancestor David."

As an adult, Jesus was baptized by John the Baptist, a great prophet and preacher who was preparing the way for Jesus. Upon Jesus' baptism, the Christian scriptures say that heaven opened and the Holy Spirit came down upon Jesus. Then a voice from heaven said, "You are my Son, the Beloved, with you I am well pleased."

Jesus began to draw a large following as he went across the country healing people, teaching about the ways to follow God, performing miracles and preaching about the kingdom of God being established on Earth. Many followers began to wonder if Jesus was the messiah—the leader the Jewish people had been waiting for to liberate them from Roman rule and to restore the Jewish nation. Jesus had twelve disciples who were his inner circle, as well as a wider following of women and men who were devoted to him. His ministry attracted many people who were the outcasts of the time, such as the poor, people who were called sinners, and tax collectors. His ministry was aimed at reconciling all people to God. Above all else, he preached two commandments: "Love God, and love your neighbor as yourself."

As Jesus' ministry grew more prominent, the authorities decided that Jesus was a threat to stability and should be put to death. One night, after a traditional seder with his disciples, now known as the Last Supper, Jesus was captured by Roman guards who were led to him by a disciple, Judas, who betrayed him. Jesus was condemned to death and crucified on a cross. Christians believe that, in dying on the cross, Jesus revealed God's self-giving love for humankind and demonstrated a perfect human love for God and for all people. Some Christians see Jesus' death as a sacrifice that reconciled sinful humanity with God. For the followers of Jesus, this was the saddest of days because the person they believed to be the messiah was dead.

According to Christian scriptures, after three days Jesus appeared in the flesh to the women who were coming to tend to his corpse. Christians believe that God resurrected Jesus, and that by rising, Jesus conquered sin, oppression, death and suffering. The resurrected Jesus appeared to the disciples, and so the ministry of Jesus continued through the work of the disciples after Jesus ascended to join God in heaven.

Jesus continued to appear to people on Earth—most famously to a man named Saul who had been intent on persecuting Jesus' followers. Jesus came to Saul on the road to Damascus, blinded him and asked Saul why he was persecuting him. After encountering Jesus, Saul repented of his own sins and persecution and became a Christian. Saul's name was changed to Paul, and he became the most famous follower of Jesus and the author of many of the letters that are in the Christian scriptures. The defining feature of a Christian continues to be someone who, like Paul, has encountered Jesus in his or her life and been transformed into a follower, identifying him or herself as a Christian.

Sacred texts

The Bible is the name for the collection of Christian sacred texts. The first section is called the Old Testament and consists of the thirty-nine books of the Hebrew scriptures, which Christians view as sacred. The second section is called the New Testament and is made up of twenty-seven books about Jesus' life and teachings and the significance of his birth, death and resurrection. The New Testament books are generally emphasized within Christian church worship services and private devotion.

The Gospels (which means "good news") at the beginning of the New Testament contain the sayings of Jesus as well as the stories of his life, death and resurrection as told by four authors: Mark, Matthew, Luke and John. The acts of the apostles and the letters of Saint Paul are in the second half of the New Testament, and they are essentially advice written to the earliest churches around the Mediterranean on how to follow Jesus Christ.

HINDUISM

Helpful terms

Avatar—incarnation of a Hindu deity

Bhajan—hymns or chants

Bhakta—a worshiper of God, a follower of the Hindu path

Bindi—red mark applied on the forehead by a Hindu woman

Darshan—exchange between the Divine and human in worship, literally "seeing"

Guru—spiritual teacher

Moksha—liberation from the cycle of reincarnation

Murti—a picture or statue representation of a god to be found in a shrine at home or at the temple

Mantra—a sacred word or phrase often assigned by a guru to a disciple

Namaste—gesture of greeting and respect made by pressing palms together in front of the chest

Prasad—food used for devotional purposes

Puja—religious ritual, offering

Sadhu—someone who renounces the world to concentrate on the spiritual disciplines

Samsara—world of illusion, the cycle of reincarnation

Seva—charitable service or activism, unselfish work

Sri—Lord

Where should I go?

Hindu temples and centers can be found across the United States and Canada. Look in the *Yellow Pages* under "Religion" or "Churches" to see if any are listed in your area. If not, enter "Hindu Temples" and the name of your state into your favorite Internet search engine. Once you locate a temple, call to ask what day of the week would be best for a visit—generally Saturdays are the best day. Ask if anyone from the temple could show you around. Most often, staff or members of the temple are happy to help you plan a visit. Go with a friend to have someone to share the experience with you.

What should I wear?

Visitors should dress respectfully when visiting a Hindu temple. Wear modest, comfortable clothing that looks good. Guys should wear dress pants with a button-down shirt, and girls should wear nice slacks and a blouse, or a long dress. Do not show your midriff, or wear short skirts or shorts. Because you will be taking off your shoes, either wear sandals (and go barefoot in the temple) or be sure to put on clean socks or hose before you go.

Should I bring money?

You should bring a little bit of money to be put in the collection boxes labeled with the word *hundi* or *dakshina*, which helps maintain the temple.

What will I see?

A Hindu temple does not have a single focus of worship in the front of the room like a church, mosque or synagogue. Instead, several types of devotion can occur at the same time. Priests perform *pujas* (religious ceremonies) in connection to the deities. A priest may also be performing *puja* for private family rituals. An important ritual is bathing the image of the god or goddess with milk and honey, a rite performed only by priests. After the bathing, the attendees will experience *darshan*, or a vision of the god or goddess, which is said to give great power for those present.

You may notice some individuals engaged in private devotion, reciting the names of the god being honored. Vishnu, for instance, has one thousand names and to recite them all takes about an hour.

Some people may have red powder on their foreheads. You'll see people patting their face, or lightly knocking their forehead, prostrate on the ground or standing upright with their hands in a prayer position—all ways of showing devotion. After showing devotion, people will circle the altar clockwise. People tend to come and go as they please and take personal responsibility for their own ritual and spiritual life.

You may wish to bring a small gift for the god or goddess of the temple if you want to indicate respect for the practices of Hinduism. Most common are pieces of fruit or some flowers. There is no eating inside the temple, so don't bring food that is not meant as an offering. Take a seat on the side with your legs crossed and maintain a respectful silence. If you want to experience the temple in a devotional way put a dot of the red powder called *kum kum* on your forehead using your right hand ring finger to apply the dot. *Kum kum* can be found in bowls around the temple. A good rule to remember is to always use your right hand for everything. If you've brought flowers, offer them to the priest with a respectful smile and nod. Do not speak to him or extend your hand to be shaken, as they are busy with the ritual aspects of the temple.

While in this sacred place, you may wish to silently chant a *mantra* (repeated words) of devotion. Don't get too close to the deity as only priests are allowed to go onto the altars. *Turn off your cell phone!*

Religious observances

Navaratri/Durga Puja

This joyous festival lasts for nine nights. It is dedicated to the three main female manifestations of God in Hinduism: Parvati (or Durga, the goddess of valor), Lakshmi (goddess of wealth) and Sarasvati (goddess of knowledge and art).

Diwali (Hindu and Sikh)

The five-day Diwali festival, known as the Festival of Lights, commemorates Lord Rama's return to his kingdom, Ayodhya, after fourteen years of exile. Diwali is a national holiday in India, often celebrated as the new year and, in many places, the end of the business year. Houses across India are thoroughly cleaned and brightly lit to welcome in Lakshmi, the goddess of wealth and prosperity.

Holi

The spring celebration of Holi commemorates the victory of the god Vishnu over Hiranyakasipu, a demon king. One of the favorite holidays of India's north, Holi includes devotional elements, but is largely known for the practice of smearing paint in many colors on neighbors and strangers alike. The night before Holi there is a large bonfire and the next morning the playing with colors begins with everyone shouting "Happy Holi!" The holiday concludes with large gatherings of family and friends at people's homes.

Ganesh Chaturthi

This ten-day holiday celebrates the birth of the Hindu god Ganesha, the elephant-headed god of wisdom and "remover of obstacles." Families who celebrate this festival install and decorate a Ganesh idol, traditionally made of clay, in their home.

Basic tenets

Hinduism is the oldest of the world's major religions, and also the most diverse. Hinduism is known for its religious tolerance, seeing truth in many different spiritual paths. The term "Hinduism" does not describe one specific religious doctrine, but is broadly used to describe religious traditions developed in India over the past 3,500 years. In modern-day India, different regions have their own unique rituals and customs. While most Hindus recognize all the deities, the Hindus in different regions emphasize different gods as the primary focus of their devotion.

Hinduism has no prophet or great teacher who uniquely conveyed Hindu beliefs as Christ did for Christianity or the Buddha for Buddhism. However, Hindus do hold many beliefs in common. Hindus believe in Brahman, the supreme reality who is everything and everywhere in the universe. In essence, Brahman is the equivalent of the English word "God" in the ancient Indian language of Sanskrit. There are many deities, male and female, who personify Brahman's various attributes, and Hindus worship at personal shrines and temples dedicated to these gods and goddesses. Because of this multitude of personifications, many people think Hinduism is a polytheistic faith, or one that worships more than one Supreme Being. But Diana Eck, a professor at Harvard, suggests we look at these various deities like the pattern in a kaleidoscope—each reflecting an aspect of God (*A New Religious America*).

While Brahman is the supreme reality of all things, each person has within him or her *atman*, which is the infinite, or true self that is connected to God. *Atman* should not be confused with our Western idea of ego or the finite self. *Atman*, or our infinite self, gets reborn from one lifetime to the next in a process called reincarnation. It can be helpful in trying to understand these concepts to think of *atman* as someone playing a chess game. In chess, a player can lose pieces and even lose the match, but isn't defined completely by that match, or by a specific chessboard. Instead, he or she will endure to play another game. We can envision reincarnation in the same way. Our infinite selves are not defined by this life, or this reality, and we too may endure to live another time. Another way to understand reincarnation is to think of a shirt we've outgrown. We shed our bodies when we have outgrown them, and get new bodies to house the infinite self or *atman* in the next life.

The infinite self is reincarnated through many different lifetimes. Each person's new position and situation depends on the karma she or he created in the previous life. Through actions, words and deeds, the individual creates his or her own destiny. The fulfillment of *dharma*, which is duty and good conduct, is how each person creates positive karma. One important principle in *dharma* is *ahimsa*, or not doing injury to living beings, including animals; that is why many Hindus are vegetarians. Ultimately, the goal of Hindus is to be liberated (*moksha*) from the cycle of reincarnation (*samsara*) and to join completely with Brahman (God).

Gods and Goddesses

Each of the Hindu deities represents a face of Brahman. Here's an introduction to the attributes of a few of the most important gods and goddesses of Hinduism:

Lord Brahma is called the Creator of the Universe. He is the first member of the Hindu Trinity that also includes Lord Vishnu and Lord Shiva.

Goddess Sarasvati is the female companion of Lord Brahma and is the goddess of knowledge.

Lord Vishnu preserves and sustains the universe when evil threatens. Lord Vishnu appears in various forms known as *Avatars*. Krishna and Rama are two of Lord Vishnu's best-known *Avatars*, or incarnations.

Goddess Lakshmi is the wife of Lord Vishnu and the goddess of wealth and prosperity—both material and spiritual.

Lord Ganesha removes obstacles and helps gain success in human endeavors.

Lord Shiva dissolves or destroys in order to create anew in the cyclic process of creation in the universe.

Parvati is the wife of Lord Shiva. She often appears riding a tiger as the warrior goddess, or as Kali, who wears a skull necklace.

Sacred texts

The Hindu tradition is found in the wisdom of thousands of years of scriptures, teachers and in ritual observances.

The most sacred of the Hindu texts are the Vedas: Rig Veda, Sama Veda, Yajur Veda and Atharva Veda. These four books contain creation stories, hymns, wisdom and rituals. The oldest of the Vedas was composed in 1500 BCE and is considered one of the world's most ancient religious writings.

A second major set of texts after the Vedas are the Upanishads, composed between 800 and 400 BCE. Also known as Vedanta, they contain much of the religious philosophy that we think of as Hinduism today.

The Bhagavad Gita is the most famous of the Hindu scriptures. It records Lord Krishna's advice to the warrior Arjuna before a war begins. Lord Krishna, as Arjuna's chariot driver, teaches on the nature of reincarnation and how to stop the cycle of rebirth to achieve liberation. The Bhagavad Gita is part of a larger text, a massive epic poem called the Mahabharata, which was composed about 400 BCE. Another epic religious poem is the Ramayana, which details the life of Lord Ram who is an incarnation of Vishnu.

ISLAM

Helpful terms

Adhan—call to prayer

Halal—lawful, often used when talking about dietary requirements

Haram—unlawful

Hijab—the traditional head covering for Muslim women

Imam—a religious leader or teacher, especially at jumma

Jumma—Friday communal prayer

Masjid, Mosque—a house of worship where Muslims gather for community prayer

Mihrab—curve in the wall that indicates the direction of Mecca for purpose of prayer

Muazinne—someone who chants the Qur'an

Musallah—prayer room

Rak'ah—the cycle of prayer that includes physical motions and verbal prayer

Sheikh—teacher

Surah—a chapter

'Umma—a Muslim community

Wudu/wadu—ritual cleansing of hands, face and feet before prayer

Where should I go?

While *salat* (daily prayer) is usually a private matter, Muslims congregate at the mosque or *masjid* on Fridays around noon or 1 P.M. for weekly communal prayer called *jumma*. Jumma is the best time to experience Muslim community and witness Islamic worship. The phone book or the Web site *www.islamicfinder.org* will help you locate a mosque near you. Call ahead to ask if visitors are welcome and if someone might be able to greet you and be an informal host. If you have a Muslim friend, ask if you can go with her or him—it will be a great way to become better friends. If not, take a non-Muslim friend so someone will share the experience with you.

What should I wear?

Always dress nicely and respectably when visiting a mosque. Men should wear nice slacks with a button-down shirt. Coat and tie are not required. Women should wear a long dress or a long-sleeve blouse with a long skirt or conservative long pants. Women's clothing should cover the legs and arms, and a scarf must be worn to cover the head. Wearing symbolic jewelry such as crosses, star of David or signs of the Zodiac is not appropriate, as Islam prohibits any depiction of God.

Should I bring money?

There may be a box in which you could put a small donation, but you do not need to bring anything else.

What will I see?

At the entrance you will see a place where people have left their shoes, which are not allowed in the *musallah* (main prayer room). You may also see a place where people can perform *wudu* or *wadu*, which is the ritual washing of the face, hands and feet before prayer. There will likely be only a few chairs in the *musallah*, and they are meant for the elderly. The *musallah* will have carpets on the floor. Notice that there are no images of people or animals that could distract the worshiper from God. The *musallah* is oriented toward the city of Mecca, and Muslims always pray in that direction—look for a curved niche in the wall called the *mihrab* to find which way to pray. Prayer is coordinated with a series of ritualized motions of placing the hands on the stomach or at the side, then putting them behind the ears, then a prostration and a kneeling. Women pray separately from men, either behind them or in a completely different room. The imam will lead the prayers and give the sermon. The *muazzine* performs the call to worship when the service begins.

Arrive a bit before the service so you can take a seat before the service begins. As a non-Muslim, you should sit on the side and observe. Someone may greet you with the phrase "as salaam alaykum" (ahs SAH-lahm ah-LAY-koom), which means "peace be with you." You may wish to respond by repeating it, or you can also reply, "Wa alaykum salaam" (ah-LAY-koom ah SAH-lahm), which means "And peace also with you." Muslim prayers are in Arabic, and you won't likely be familiar with the accompanying positions. The best thing to do is observe with a respectful reverence for the faith that you are witnessing. There is a time when Muslims will pass the peace with a handshake or touching the heart. You should return this gesture in the same way and pass the peace back. Women will often not shake hands, but you may touch your heart in a respectful way. Do not talk during the service, especially while the imam is speaking or while the *muazzine* is performing the call to worship. *Turn off your cell phone!*

Basic tenets

Islam is a monotheistic (one God) religion, along with Judaism and Christianity. These three religions are sometimes grouped together as the "Abrahamic" religions, because of their common patriarch, Abraham. Muslims worship the same God as the Jews and Christians, Allah being the Arabic word for God.

Islam also acknowledges many prophets and leaders of Jewish and Christian history, such as Adam, Noah, Abraham, Moses and Jesus. Muslims believe that the line of prophets culminates in the Prophet Muhammad, known as the Last Prophet. The Prophet Muhammad was born in Mecca in the year 570 CE, in present-day Saudi Arabia. He had the final revelation of God as recorded in the Qur'an (or Koran).

The word "Islam" means to submit to the will of God, and is rooted in the Arabic word for "peace"—the peace that comes from submitting to God's will. God's will is understood through reading and following the Qur'an. As Christians believed that God took human form in the person of Jesus Christ, Muslims believe that God was revealed in pure form through the Qur'an, which was conveyed to the Prophet Muhammad. The Qur'an is very specific about the nature of God and how God requires Muslims to live by worship and by deeds of faith.

Muhammad

The Prophet Muhammad is so deeply admired by Muslims that it is correct after saying his name to add the phrase: "Blessings and peace be upon him." While the name Muhammad means "highly praised," the Prophet Muhammad is not considered a divine being. For Muslims, the Prophet Muhammad is the most important prophet and a man who lived his life in an exemplary way.

The Prophet Muhammad was born in Mecca in the year 570. He was orphaned at an early age and raised by his uncle's tribe, one of the most influential of the city. His own losses made him sensitive to the needs of others, especially the poor and orphaned, and he was of a pure heart and gentle disposition. He began to work for a wealthy widow named Khadija, a businesswoman whom he eventually married and who was an important source of comfort for him. Muhammad began to spend time meditating in the Cave of Hira near the summit of the Mountain of Light near Mecca. At the age of forty, he received the first revelation from God through the Angel Gabriel, who appeared to him in the cave now commemorated by Muslims as the Night of Power. Over the next twenty-three years, God revealed the Qur'an to Muhammad, which he committed to memory.

Muhammad began to recite (the word "Qur'an" comes from the Arabic word "recite") the words that had been revealed to him and to preach about the one God: "There is no god but God" ("La ilaha illa 'llah!"). His monotheism clashed with the polytheistic (multigod) beliefs of the people of Mecca. His teaching that all people were equal also raised suspicion among the rulers of Mecca, whose power depended in part on the sharp class distinctions of the time. The leaders also disliked the Prophet Muhammad because he preached a strong morality to a violent and decadent society.

In 622, amid growing hostility from the leaders of Mecca, the prophet Muhammad was invited by the leaders of another desert city named Medina to govern their people. Muhammad was told by God to accept, and his migration, known as the *hijra*, marks the beginning of the Muslim calendar to this day. Muhammad had great success in governing Medina. There he built the first mosque, set up an Islamic code for social order and became renowned for his just administration of the city.

A period of war began between the people of Mecca and the followers of Muhammad in Medina. Muhammad ultimately prevailed and returned to Mecca where he dealt mercifully with his former enemies. An important symbol of Mecca was the Ka'ba, the large, square temple that Muslims believe was originally built by Abraham and his son Ishmael, but which was being used as a temple for pagan worship. On his return to Mecca, Muhammad accepted the mass conversion of the people and rededicated the Ka'ba to God.

Muhammad lived to see Islam established throughout Arabia, creating a peace that had been unknown in a region torn apart by warlords. Within one hundred years of the prophet's death, Islam had spread throughout what is now known as the Middle East, to Spain and as far east as Afghanistan, China and India.

Sacred texts

The Qur'an, which literally means "recitation," was revealed in perfect grammar and poetic beauty to the Prophet Muhammad over the course of twenty-three years by the Angel Gabriel and is Islam's most sacred text. The perfection of the Qur'an is considered a miracle since Muhammad could barely write his name. Arabic is still considered the only language in which one can truly understand the Qur'an, as all efforts to translate it into other languages are merely considered "interpretations." The Qur'an is divided into 114 chapters (*surahs*) that are arranged in decreasing length excepting the first and most important chapter called the Al-Fatiha, which is recited as the opening of prayer.

The *hadith* is the collection of the deeds and sayings of the Prophet Muhammad that are also considered sacred texts as they are examples of the model behavior and practice of the prophet.

The Five Pillars

The five requirements for the Muslim's life are known as the Five Pillars of Islam.

1. **The Creed** (*Shahada*): To call oneself a Muslim you must believe in your heart and publicly proclaim in Arabic: "There is no god but God,

and Muhammad is the messenger of God." This creed reinforces the belief that nothing shares divinity with God and only God is deserving of worship.

2. **Prayer** (*Salat*): An observant Muslim prays five times a day: at dawn, noon, mid-afternoon, dusk and evening. Prayers are always said in Arabic. The prayers can be said either alone or in community. Friday noon is the traditional time for a communal service at the masjid (also known as mosque), the Muslim building of worship. The faithful pray facing Mecca, kneeling, standing and bowing in a sequence that is part of the formal ritual. Salat constantly puts the Muslim in direct communication with God throughout the day and maintains God's rightful, primary place in the Muslim's life.

3. **Alms Giving** (*Zakat*): Each Muslim is expected to give away 2½ percent of his or her assets if they are financially able. This money is distributed to members of the community who are in need. Not only does this benefit the poor, but zakat also benefits the ones who give by freeing them of greed and selfishness and the risk of worshiping possessions rather than God.

4. **The Ramadan Fast** (*Sawm*): During Ramadan, the most sacred month in the Muslim lunar calendar, Muslims refrain from all food, drink and sexual activity from sunrise to sundown. Ramadan focuses the Muslim's mind on God and is also a time of identification with the poor.

5. **Pilgrimage** (*Hajj*): If physically or financially able, all Muslims must make a pilgrimage to Mecca, the birthplace of Muhammad in what is now Saudi Arabia. As people of different races, classes and genders come together at Mecca, the Hajj is a symbol of equality before God.

The Holy Month of Ramadan

Muslims fast between dawn and sunset during this month-long obser-vance. The fast requires abstaining from water, food, smoking and sexual activity during daylight hours. The month of fasting is seen as a time of con-templation to repent sins and to acknowledge the blessings of life and be grateful to Allah. Each evening, Muslims gather together to break the fast with a special evening meal called *iftar*. Many Muslims will read the entire Qur'an during Ramadan.

Eid-ul-Fitr (the "Festival of the Breaking of the Fast")

This important festival marks the end of Ramadan, the month of fasting, and is marked by alms giving and great feasts.

Hajj

Hajj is the pilgrimage to Mecca that all Muslims who are financially or physically able should make at least once a lifetime. Pilgrims make a circuit around the Ka'ba, the square temple that Muhammad rededicated to God upon his return to Mecca.

Eid-ul-Adha

The Feast of Sacrifice, which is celebrated by those on Hajj, as well as those who are at home. To commemorate the obedience of the prophet Abraham, who was asked by God to sacrifice his son, a sheep or goat is sacrificed for a feast shared by friends and family and providing food for the poor. Eid-ul-Adha also marks the end of the Hajj.

Hijra

The first day of the Islamic New Year, Hijra (also called Hegira) is the anniversary of the Prophet Muhammad's migration, in the year 622, from Mecca, his birthplace, to Medina, where he built the first mosque and estab-lished the Islamic code of practice and social order. It is a day of celebration of the beginning of the Muslim community.

JUDAISM

If you visit:

Helpful terms

Bimah—the area of the synagogue or temple where the rabbi and cantor lead

Cantor—leads the congregation in singing the prayers

Davening—praying with accompanying motions

Halakhah—the code of conduct, law or way

Mehitsah—the screen, wall or sheet used to divide the women and men in Orthodox congregations

Minyan—ten or more people (men in Orthodox Judaism) gathered together as the minimum requirement for a prayer service

Mitzvah—commandment

Rabbi—teacher and spiritual leader; while the rabbi often leads the worship service, any adult person can technically lead the service

Sabbath—day of rest and worship that happens from sunset on Friday to sunset on Saturday

Siddur—prayer book

Synagogue—a building for the purpose of worship and the study of Judaism

Tallit—prayer shawl

Yarmulke/Kippah—the skull cap traditionally worn by males

Where should I go?

Jewish temples and synagogues number in the thousands in this country, and there is likely one in your hometown. The best way to experience a new religion is with a friend, so if you have a Jewish friend, ask if you could go with her or him to a service sometime. If not, look in the *Yellow Pages* under "Religion," and you will find several listings for synagogues or Jewish temples. Call ahead to see if visitors are welcome—they generally are. Most services are held on Friday evenings around sunset or on Saturday mornings—call for times. If you're unfamiliar with Hebrew, you might want to pick a Reform service, which uses more English during the service than Conservative or Orthodox congregations. Most synagogues, however, have prayer books with English translations.

What should I wear?

Though dress codes vary, as a visitor you should always dress respectably. In Reform and Conservative synagogues, guys should wear long dress pants with a polo or button-down shirt—coat and tie are optional. Women should wear nice slacks or modest skirts with a blouse. In Orthodox synagogues, guys should wear a coat and tie, and women should wear long skirts that cover their legs and a blouse that covers their arms. In a Conservative or Orthodox temple men will be required to wear a yarmulke or kippah inside the sanctuary. One will be provided for you at the entrance. If you are wearing religious jewelry such as a cross or any other symbol, put it inside your shirt.

What will I see?

The most important focus of every sanctuary is the ark—a cabinet that houses the Torah. The Torah is a scroll upon which the holy scriptures are written in Hebrew. Right above the ark is the eternal lamp, which remains permanently lighted. As a sign of reverence, the congregation will stand when the ark is opened or when the Torah is being carried. You may also observe the congregation turning in one direction to pray—they are turning toward Jerusalem. In Orthodox and Conservative services, prayers and reading from the Torah are mostly in Hebrew, although there are often English translations available in many *siddurs* (prayer books). Remember that Hebrew is read from right to left on the page, and similarly books begin at the right-hand cover side and proceed to the left. The Torah is read during *Shabbat* morning services, as well as on Mondays and Thursdays.

Should I bring money?

There is never a collection for money at a service. Synagogues fund themselves through membership, and you are welcome as a guest.

What should I do?

If you attend with a friend, or have called ahead, you'll likely have someone who can explain what is happening. If not, you may wish to introduce yourself to the person who greets you at the entrance by telling them that you are visiting and give them the opportunity to make you feel welcome. Members of the congregation may greet you with "Shabbat shalom," which means "Have a peaceful Sabbath." You may wish to say this back to them or say, "Thank you." Sit down anywhere you like, but if you are attending an Orthodox service remember to sit on the appropriate side for your gender.

Stay alert and stand when the congregation stands, for instance when the ark is opened, and turn when the congregation turns, for instance during the prayer toward Jerusalem. You will appreciate a lot by simply listening to the beauty of the music sung by the cantor in Hebrew and the talk in English offered by the rabbi. In the prayer book you will find what the congregation is singing in Hebrew translated into English.

Turn off your cell phone!

Basic tenets

Though Jews today have different forms of religious expression, all of Judaism is grounded in monotheism and devotion to the one God as proclaimed in the Sh'ma: "Hear, O Israel, the Lord is Our God, the Lord is One." While there is no single faith statement, all Jews agree that the story of the Jewish people is important. Even completely secular (nonreligious) Jews will celebrate the various holidays that retell this important communal history.

Judaism's most important stories involve the covenant or agreement that God made with the Jewish people starting with the patriarch Abraham, whom both Islam and Christianity also claim as their patriarch. Abraham obeyed God's call to move his family to a land that God provided for him. In exchange, God promised to bless Abraham and make a great nation of his descendants. Abraham's son, Isaac, and grandson, Jacob (whose name was changed to Israel), are also considered patriarchs of the Jewish people.

Centuries after God's promises to Abraham, the Jewish people were living enslaved in Egypt. The Egyptian pharaoh ordered all young Jewish boys to be put to death, lest the Jews grow too powerful and revolt. In defiance of the decree, one mother hid her baby son in a basket and placed it in the Nile River. The baby was found by the pharaoh's own daughter, who named the child Moses and raised him as her own. When Moses became a young man he saw a Jewish man being beaten by an Egyptian. Angered, he killed the Egyptian man and fled to the desert.

There, God told Moses to return to and free his people from captivity. God aided the Jews' exodus from slavery: first by sending plagues when the pharaoh refused Moses' demand that he let the Jewish people go, then later by parting the Red Sea so the Jews could make their escape. For the next forty years the Jews wandered in the desert. During that time God presented the Jews with the sacred covenant that promised if the Jews obeyed God's commandments they would be blessed. God then revealed the Ten Commandments to Moses on Mount Sinai. These commandments form the core of the Jewish ethical code and are the basis for much of Western culture's understanding of morality. These are ten of the 613 laws, statutes and judgments in Judaism called Mitzvot or commandments.

The Ten Commandments are:

1. I am the Lord your God, who has taken you out of the land of Egypt, from the house of slavery.
2. You shall have no other gods but me.
3. You shall not take the name of your Lord in vain.
4. You shall remember and keep the Sabbath day holy.
5. Honor your father and mother.
6. You shall not kill.
7. You shall not commit adultery.
8. You shall not steal.
9. You shall not bear false witness against your neighbor.
10. You shall not covet (desire) your neighbors' goods. You shall not covet your neighbors' house. You shall not covet your neighbors' wife, servant, bull, donkey, nor anything that is your neighbors'.

When the Jews entered into the land God had promised them, called Canaan, they established a kingdom there. King David was the most famous of Jewish kings, and his son, Solomon, built the temple in Jerusalem in the year 950 BCE to honor and worship God. In addition to threats from neighboring countries, there were internal struggles within the Jewish society. God selected certain people as prophets (which means "to speak for") who were concerned with how well the Jewish people were following the religious rules of God, as well as the society's morality, especially the treatment of the poor. This combination of religious observance with concern for the poor is an important aspect of Jewish culture and religious belief to this day.

Twice the temple that the Jews built in Jerusalem to honor and worship God was destroyed: first by the Babylonians in 586 BCE and later by the Romans in 70 CE. After the destruction of the second temple, the Jewish nation dissolved. In what is called the Diaspora, the Jews were scattered around what is now known as the Middle East, and Europe. With the temple gone, the tradition of rabbis or teachers became essential for the continued practice and teaching of the religion and development of Jewish thought and identity through writing the *Mishna*, and the Babylonian and Palestinian Talmuds.

During the Diaspora, two major branches of Judaism developed: Ashkenazi and Sephardic. The Ashkenazi Jews settled in central and eastern Europe and Russia and were influenced by those cultures. One part of the Ashkenazi heritage is the Yiddish language, a combination of Hebrew and German. The Sephardic Jews settled in Spain and Portugal, as well as in the Middle East. Each of these two groups has contributed its unique traditions to general Jewish culture and rabbinic knowledge and wisdom worldwide.

Perhaps the most powerful influence on Jews and Judaism in recent times is the attempted extermination of the Jews by Nazis in Germany before and during World War II, commonly referred to as the Holocaust. More than six million Jews were killed from the late 1930s to the middle 1940s—close to one-third of all the Jews in the world at that time. This horrific tragedy accelerated the efforts of those people who had been attempting to establish a homeland for the Jews since the end of the nineteenth century. In 1948 the State of Israel was created. In Israel, various forms of Jewish life, from ultra-orthodox to completely secular, coexist. Approximately one-third of all Jews now live in Israel.

The Hebrew Bible, called the Tanach, consists of twenty-four books, divided into three sections. The first section, called the Torah, is the most important. The Torah is treated with extreme reverence. It consists of five books: Genesis, Exodus, Leviticus, Numbers and Deuteronomy.

The second section of the Hebrew Bible is called the Neviim, which means "the prophets," and the third is called the Ketuvim, or "the writings," including the Psalms and Proverbs. The Hebrew Bible is the basis for what Christians call the Old Testament, although translations can sometimes be different and several books appear in the Tanach that are not in the Christian Bible.

Other important sacred texts within Judaism are the Talmud and the Midrash. These constitute what is known as the Oral Law because they were originally passed down orally from generation to generation. These texts were created and written down by rabbis, religious scholars and teachers who continued to study and write about the Torah and Jewish custom and law during the time of the Diaspora.

Religious observances

Rosh Hashanah

Rosh Hashanah is the Jewish New Year. The holiday is marked by the blowing of a ram's horn, called the *shofar*. Jews celebrate by attending synagogue and festive meals and eating traditional foods like apples and honey to represent a sweet new year. Falling some time in September or October, Rosh Hashanah marks the beginning of a ten-day period of reflection, repentance and spiritual renewal that culminates with Yom Kippur.

Yom Kippur

Yom Kippur is known as the Day of Atonement. Jews confess and repent of sins of the past year and ask forgiveness from God and from those they have committed sins against. Jews believe that their fate for the next year is sealed on Yom Kippur. The day is marked by fasting (no eating or drinking), refraining from work and attending prayer services. Yom Kippur and Rosh

Hashanah, together with the festive holidays of Sukkot and Simchat Torah, are known as the Judaism High Holidays.

Sukkot

Called the Festival of Booths, Sukkot is a harvest celebration. Jews erect wooden structures called *sukkot*, or booths, to commemorate the huts that the Israelites dwelled in during their forty years in the desert after the exodus from Egypt. The festival also celebrates God's protection of the Israelites during this time.

Simchat Torah

Simchat Torah literally means "joy of the Torah." Falling immediately after Sukkot, it marks the end of the cycle of annual Torah reading, and the restarting of this cycle by reading the first chapter of Genesis. It is a very festive holiday, when Jews dance joyfully with the Torah scrolls in the synagogue and often in the street.

Chanukah

Known as the Festival of Lights, Chanukah commemorates the victory of Judah Maccabee, a pious Jew, over the Hellenizing influences of and oppression by the Greek government. During the eight days of the Chanukah, candles are lit to remember the miracle of the great Temple lamp burning for eight nights although there was only enough oil for one.

Purim

Purim is the celebration of the saving of the Jews through the courage of Queen Esther who bravely stood up for Jewish people as told in the Book of Esther in the Hebrew Bible.

Passover (Pesach)

This important holiday remembers the exodus of the Jews from slavery in Egypt. Jews do not eat bread or any food made with yeast to remind them of the haste with which their ancestors escaped from Egypt. They eat a special flat, unleavened bread called *matzoh* instead. At the ritual meal, called a *seder*, the story of the exodus is told, and Jews eat special food symbolizing the Israelites' experience in Egypt.

Shavuot

Shavuot is the Hebrew word for "weeks" and is a joyful festival that falls seven weeks after the end of Passover and celebrates the receiving of the Ten Commandments and the Torah. It also recalls the spring harvest in Israel and the bringing of first fruits to the Temple in Jerusalem.

Tisha B'Av

A day of mourning, marking the destruction of the first and second Temple in Jerusalem. The day also commemorates other tragedies that the Jewish people have endured. It is a day of fasting, and Jews also refrain from washing and wearing leather shoes. The book of Lamentations is read in synagogue.

WARNING: CULTS

Religious exploration and spiritual seeking is a wonderful journey. But as in any adventure, there are dangers. Most spiritual and religious groups are perfectly healthy, but it pays to be aware of how some can be unhealthy. Trust your gut, and if you have a bad feeling about anyone or any group, remember you're absolutely free to walk away, and you have the right to be left alone. In general, watch out for individuals or groups who:

- Don't give a clear answer about who they are, what their credentials are and what they represent;
- Don't tolerate critical or independent thinking by you or anyone outside the organization;
- Are immediately overwhelmingly friendly;
- Want to isolate you from your friends and family;
- You hardly know who try to give you gifts or other tokens of friendship with no strings attached;
- Can't take "no" for an answer and try to prevent leaving, or make you feel guilty for rejecting them;
- Immediately involve you in intense recruitment and proselytizing;
- Offer magical solutions to your problems;
- Make unrealistic demands on the use of your time or personal finances;
- Want to control your daily life or way of looking at things; and
- Are excessively judgmental about your life or faith.

Again, while most religious leaders are great people who are living good lives based on the religious tenets of their faith, some adults abuse their religious authority to create inappropriate relationships with young people in their care. This is against the law, and also goes against the beliefs of every religion, and you should not allow it.

Here are some rules of behavior that every religious leader should be following. If you feel these rules are being broken, inform your parents or someone else you trust immediately.

- Any physical contact by a religious leader should always be nonsexual, nonviolent and appropriate.
- You should never accept an invitation alone to a private residence of any religious clergy.
- You should never be offered a drink or drugs by a religious leader.
- You should never be given expensive gifts by a religious leader unless your parents have been informed.
- On a retreat or overnight you should never be required to share a bed with an adult.

INTERFAITH YOUTH CORE CODE OF CONDUCT

The goals of Interfaith Youth Core (*www.ifyc.org*) programs are to:

- Help strengthen the religious identities of participating youth;
- Build understanding and respect between diverse religious youth and their faith communities; and
- Encourage cooperation between diverse religious youth and their faith communities.

Code of Conduct

- Your role in interfaith dialogue is to 1) learn about religions, customs and practices that are different from your own; and 2) represent your own faith tradition with love and respect. Active, respectful conversation is the tool with which you will both learn and teach.
- Conduct yourself in a way that demonstrates both your pride in your faith and your commitment to inter-religious respect.
- Do not try to convert other people to your faith tradition.
- Do not debate the superiority of your beliefs or practices over others. This will push us away from one another.
- Be aware that practitioners of some faiths will not make direct eye contact or shake hands with members of the other sex. They may only be able to eat certain types of food, pray at specific times of the day or observe a different day of the week than you. There will also be differences in how strictly people practice. Try not to judge people for these differences.
- Many of your rituals, customs and beliefs will be unfamiliar to others. You may be asked questions about things that seem obvious. Please take time to answer these questions thoroughly and thoughtfully. Similarly, ask your own most basic questions—you can expect others to respond thoughtfully.
- Don't forget to enjoy yourself and encourage others to have fun with you.

WHERE TO GO FOR MORE INFORMATION

Baha'i

On the Web

www.bahai.org (The official Web site for the Baha'i Faith)

www.bahai-youth.org (Listing of Baha'i youth groups throughout the world)

Buddhism

On the Web

www.buddhanet.net (The largest online Buddhism site)

www.tricycle.com (The Web site for *Tricycle*, an excellent Buddhist magazine)

www.dalailama.com (The Web site for the Dalai Lama)

www.wfby.org (The Web site for the World Fellowship of Buddhist Youth)

On the Big Screen

Seven Years in Tibet, 1997 (PG-13). Starring: Brad Pitt; Director: Jean-Jacques Annaud

The Cup Phörpa, 1999 (G). Starring: Orgyen Tobgyal; Director: Khyentse Norbu

Little Buddha, 1993 (PG). Starring: Keanu Reeves; Director: Bernardo Bertolucci

Chasing Buddha (documentary), 2000. Director: Amiel Courtin-Wilson

In Your Headphones

Mantra Mix: Tibetan Benefit Album, Narada World Label, includes works by Madonna, REM, Moby and many others, as well as companion CD of music by Buddhist monks and his Holiness the Dalai Lama

Beastie Boys, *Check Your Head*, Grand Royal Label. Special tracks to look for are "Gratitude," "Stand Together" and "Namaste."

On the Web

www.relevantmagazine.com (Relevant media. A Web site and magazine for
Gen-X Christians)

www.youmagazine.com (Catholic Youth Online)

www.taize.fr (Taize community)

www.bustedhalo.com (A cool Catholic site)

www.wcc-coe.org/wcc/english.html (The World Council of Churches Web
site with listings of churches around the world)

www.oca.org (The Web site for the Orthodox Church of America)

On the Big Screen

Jonah: A Veggie Tales Movie, 2002. Directors: Mike Nawrocki, Phil Vischer

The Ten Commandments, 1956. Starring: Charlton Heston; Director: Cecil
B. DeMille

The Apostle, 1998. Starring: Robert Duvall

Left Behind, 2001. Starring: Kirk Cameron

Bruce Almighty, 2003. Director: Tom Shadyac; Starring: Jim Carrey,
Morgan Freeman

Brother Sun, Sister Moon—The Life of St. Francis, 1973. Director: Franco
Zeffirelli

In Your Headphones:

U2, *Joshua Tree*, 1987

Ben Harper and the Innocent Criminals, *Fight for Your Mind*, 1995

P.O.D. (Payable on Death), *Satellite*, 2001

Kirk Franklin, *The Nu Nation Project*, 1998

Hinduism

On the Web

www.hindu.org (A comprehensive Hinduism site)

www.hinduyouth.com (Hindu Youth Site)

www.vedanta-newyork.org (The Web site for the Vedanta Society of New York)

www.rediff.com (Indian pop culture, Blogs and more)

In Your Headphones

Various Artists, *The Gayatri Mantra*, 2001

Ravi Shankar, *Bridges: The Best of Ravi Shankar*, 2001

DJ Cheb I Sabbah, *Shri Durga*, 1999; *MahaMaya*, 2000; and *Krishna Lila*, 2002

The Beatles, "Across the Universe," from *Let It Be*, 1970

George Harrison, "My Sweet Lord," from *All Things Must Pass*, 1970

Islam

On the Web

www.wamyusa.org (World Assembly of Muslim Youth)

www.islamicity.com (Comprehensive Muslim Web site)

www.islamonline.net/english/index.shtml (An Islamic news portal)

On the Big Screen

The Message, 1976. Director: Moustapha Akkad; Starring: Anthony Quinn

Malcolm X, 1992. Director: Spike Lee; Starring: Denzel Washington

The Lion of the Desert (Omar Mukhtar). Director: Moustapha Akkad; Starring: Anthony Quinn

Ali, 2001. Director: Michael Mann; Starring: Will Smith

In Your Headphones

Mos Def, *Black on Both Sides*, 1999
Nusrat Fateh Ali Khan, *Visions of Allah*, 1999
Yusuf Islam (Cat Stevens), *A Is for Allah*, 2000

Judaism

On the Web

www.jvibe.com (Jvibe—a Jewish site for teens)
www.jewsweek.com (*Jewsweek*, a fun weekly Jewish news magazine)
www.newvoices.org (*New Voices* magazine, a national, progressive Jewish student publication)
www.myjewishlearning.com/index.htm (My Jewish Learning, a comprehensive Jewish learning and resource site)
www.zeek.net/links.shtml (Cool online magazine with links to Jewish sites)

On the Big Screen

The Prince of Egypt, 1998 (animated)
The Pianist, 2002. Director: Roman Polanski
Hebrew Hammer, 2003. Director: Jonathan Kesselman
Radio Days, 1987. Director: Woody Allen

In Your Headphones

Jewish Rappers, *Remedy, Hip Hop Hoodios*
The Klezmatics, any CD
For a list of Jews who are musicians, check out the book *Jews Who Rock* by Guy Oseary

Sikhism

On the Web

www.5knet.com (Fun Sikh youth site including Sikh basics, a game and Punjabi e-greetings)

On the Big Screen

Bend It Like Beckham, 2002. Director: Gurinder Chadha

Wicca

On the Web

www.witchvox.com/xteen.html (Young pagan essays, a collection of essays by teens on Witchvox)
www.paganpride.org (The Pagan Pride Project)
www.circlesanctuary.org (Circle Sanctuary, publishers of *Circle* magazine and other Wiccan and pagan online resources)

On the Small Screen

TV shows, *Charmed* and *Sabrina the Teenage Witch*

Zoroastrianism

On the Web

www.avesta.org (Archives of Zoroastrian information)

Interfaith

www.beliefnet.com (Beliefnet.com)

www.ifyc.org (Interfaith Youth Core)

www.nain.org (North American Interfaith Network)

www.cpwr.org (Council for a Parliament of World Religions)

www.pluralism.org (The Pluralism Project)

www.faithandvalues.com (Faith and Values Network)

www.forusa.org (Fellowship of Reconciliation)

www.interfaithcalendar.org (Interfaith Calendar)

www.interfaith-center.org/oxford (International Interfaith Centre)

www.uri.org (United Religions Initiative)

www.religioustolerance.org (Religious Tolerance)

www.sbnetwork.com/ucs/ws/ws.cfm (World Scripture)

www.youthandreligion.org (National Study of Youth and Religion)

www.spirituality.ucla.edu (Spirituality in Higher Education)

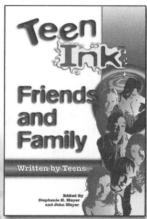

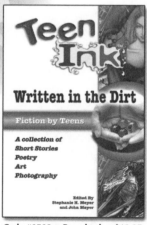